Holt Literature & Language Arts

First Course

S0-AWP-855

UNIVERSAL ACCESS **Developmental Language & Sentence Skills**

Support for the *Holt Handbook*

Guided Practice in
- **Grammar**
- **Usage**
- **Mechanics**
- **Sentences**

HOLT, RINEHART AND WINSTON

A Harcourt Classroom Education Company

Austin · New York · Orlando · Atlanta · San Francisco · Boston · Dallas · Toronto · London

STAFF CREDITS

EDITORIAL

Manager of Editorial Operations
Bill Wahlgren

Executive Editor
Robert R. Hoyt

Senior Editor
Marcia L. Kelley

Project Editor
Eric Estlund

Writing and Editing

Guy Guidici, Suzi A. Hunn, Kevin Lemoine, Amber M. Rigney, *Associate Editors*

Copyediting

Michael Neibergall, *Copyediting Manager;* Mary Malone, *Copyediting Supervisor;* Christine Altgelt, Joel Bourgeois, Elizabeth Dickson, Emily Force, Julie A. Hill, Julia Thomas Hu, Jennifer Kirkland, Millicent Ondras, Dennis Scharnberg, *Copyeditors*

Project Administration

Marie Price, *Managing Editor;* Lori De La Garza, *Editorial Operations Coordinator;* Heather Cheyne, Mark Holland, Marcus Johnson, Jennifer Renteria, Janet Riley, Kelly Tankersley, *Project Administration;* Ruth Hooker, Joie Pickett, Margaret Sanchez, *Word Processing*

Editorial Permissions

Janet Harrington, *Permissions Editor*

ART, DESIGN, AND PHOTO

Graphic Services

Kristen Darby, *Manager*
Jeff Robinson, *Senior Ancillary Designer*

Image Acquisitions

Joe London, *Director;* Jeannie Taylor, *Photo Research Supervisor;* Tim Taylor, *Photo Research Supervisor;* Rick Benavides, *Photo Researcher;* Cindy Verheyden, *Senior Photo Researcher;* Elaine Tate, *Supervisor*

Cover Design

Curtis Riker, *Director*
Sunday Patterson, *Designer*

PRODUCTION/MANUFACTURING

Belinda Barbosa Lopez, *Senior Production Coordinator*
Carol Trammel, *Production Supervisor*
Beth Prevelige, *Senior Production Manager*

REVIEWERS

Michèle Beck-von-Peccoz
San Dieguito Union High School District
Encinitas, California

Mary K. Carey
Mendez Fundamental School
Santa Ana, California

ISBN 0-03-066022-X

11 12 13 14 15   1409   18 17 16 15
4500535776

Contents

Contents

Using This Workbook

The worksheets in this workbook provide instruction, practice, and reinforcement for *Holt Handbook* and *Language & Sentence Skills Practice*.

This workbook is designed to supplement *Language & Sentence Skills Practice* by providing additional instruction and practice to students who have not yet mastered the rules and topics covered in *Holt Handbook*.

You will find throughout the workbook several special features, which have been added to aid students' mastery of grammar, usage, and mechanics. The special features include notes, reminders, tips, points of instruction after instructional and exercise examples, and guided practice for the first one or two items in each exercise.

- **Notes** provide students with pertinent information related to the rule or topic covered on a given worksheet.

- **Reminders** review grammatical terms and concepts that were covered on previous worksheets.

- **Tips** provide students with tangible aids for understanding abstract concepts. These tips include mnemonic devices, identification tests, and recognition strategies.

- **Points of Instruction** explain how the rule or topic applies to the instructional and exercise examples provided.

- **Guided Practice** helps students with the first one or two items of each exercise by asking questions that guide students to the correct answer.

Teacher's Notes and an **Answer Key** are provided in a separate booklet titled *Universal Access: Developmental Language & Sentence Skills, Teacher's Notes and Answer Key.*

Symbols for Revising and Proofreading

Symbol	Example	Meaning of Symbol
≡	at Scott lake	Capitalize a lowercase letter.
/	a gift for my Uncle	Lowercase a capital letter.
∧	cost fifty cents	Insert a missing word, letter, or punctuation mark.
⌐	by their our house	Replace something.
ℱ	What day is is it?	Leave out a word, letter, or punctuation mark.
∪	recieved	Change the order of letters or words.
¶	¶The last step is	Begin a new paragraph.
⊙	Please be patient⊙	Add a period.
∧	Yes that's right.	Add a comma.

Sentence or Sentence Fragment?

1a.	A *sentence* is a word group that contains a subject and a verb and that expresses a complete thought.

When we say that a sentence expresses a complete thought, we mean that the sentence does not need any other words for it to stand alone. A sentence also begins with a capital letter and ends with a period, a question mark, or an exclamation point.

EXAMPLES Erica won two out of three games. [The subject is *Erica*, and the verb is *won*.]

What a great day we had! [The subject is *we*, and the verb is *had*.]

Have you read that book yet? [The subject is *you*, and the verb is *Have read*.]

Hand me that pen, please. [The subject *you* is understood in this imperative sentence. The verb is *Hand*.]

EXERCISE A Add capital letters and end marks to the following word groups to make them sentences. Write your answers on the lines provided.

Example 1. you will love the new theater [This word group has a subject, *you*, and a verb, *will love*. The word group also expresses a complete thought.]

You will love the new theater.
_____

1. did you see the dog with the white hair around its left eye [Which word begins the sentence? What end mark would be appropriate?]

_____

2. the Johnsons are planning a picnic this weekend

_____

3. remember to do your assignments tonight

_____

4. what a fun surprise party that was

_____

5. has Jim called yet

_____

A *sentence fragment* is a group of words that looks like a sentence but does not contain both a subject and a verb or does not express a complete thought. Sentence fragments are common in conversation but are generally not appropriate in formal writing or speaking.

SENTENCE FRAGMENT Won two out of three games. [The word group has a verb, *Won*, but it does not have a subject.]

SENTENCE Erica won two out of three games. [The word group has a subject, *Erica*, and a verb, *won*.]

SENTENCE FRAGMENT	When you get home. [The word group contains a subject, *you*, and a verb, *get*, but it does not express a complete thought.]
SENTENCE	You can call me when you get home. [The subject is *You*, and the verb is *can call*. The word group *when you get home* is added to an independent clause that expresses a complete thought.]

EXERCISE B On the line provided, write *S* if the word group is a sentence or *F* if it is a sentence fragment.

Example __F__ **1.** After we go to dinner. [This word group contains a subject, *we*, and a verb, *go*. However, the word group does not express a complete thought, so the word group is a sentence fragment.]

_____ **6.** The sisters went home. [Does this word group contain a subject and a verb? Does it express a complete thought?]

_____ **7.** The boy in her class.

_____ **8.** Sang a beautiful song at the concert.

_____ **9.** Ken built the bookshelf himself.

_____ **10.** Did what?

EXERCISE C The following items are sentence fragments. Add words to make each sentence fragment a complete sentence. Write your answers on the lines provided.

Example 1. Before you leave for the game. [This word group has a subject, *you*, and a verb, *leave*. However, the word group does not express a complete thought, so it is a sentence fragment.]

Before you leave for the game, put on a jacket.

11. Sleeps on a pillow next to my bed. [This word group is missing a subject.]

_____

12. My favorite baseball team.

_____

13. Went to the movies yesterday.

_____

14. Is a very funny person.

_____

15. What your middle name?

_____

The Subject

The Simple Subject

Sentences consist of two main parts: subjects and predicates.

1c. The *simple subject* is the main word or word group that tells *whom* or *what* the sentence is about.

> **EXAMPLES** The **smell** of fresh bread drifted into the living room. [*What* drifted into the living room? Smell did. *Smell* is the subject of the sentence.]
>
> When did your **sisters** take an art class? [*Who* took an art class? Sisters did. *Sisters* is the subject of the sentence.]

TIP The simple subject is never found after a preposition. A preposition is a word that tells the relationship of a noun or pronoun to another word in the sentence. Some common prepositions are *about, among, at, for, from, in, of, under,* and *with.* To find the simple subject, cross out any preposition and the noun or pronoun that follows it.

> **EXAMPLE** The **smell** ~~of fresh bread~~ drifted into the living room. [*Smell* is the subject, not *bread*.]

EXERCISE A Underline the simple subject in each of the following sentences.

Example 1. Does the <u>watch</u> on the table belong to Chad? [The sentence tells about *watch*.]

1. Soft music was playing on the radio. [What is the sentence about?]

2. A pile of magazines and newspapers sat in the middle of the room.

3. Several rows of flowers are beyond the fountain.

4. The four students from Seattle enjoyed their trip to the Grand Canyon.

5. Were many delicious dishes from different countries served to the guests?

The Complete Subject

The *complete subject* consists of all the words that tell *whom* or *what* a sentence is about.

> **COMPLETE SUBJECTS** **The smell of fresh bread** drifted into the living room. [What drifted into the living room? The smell of fresh bread did. *The smell of fresh bread* is the complete subject.]
>
> Near the waterfall are **some beautiful orchids.** [What objects are near the waterfall? Some beautiful orchids are. *Some beautiful orchids* is the complete subject.]

REMINDER Sometimes the simple subject is also the complete subject.

> **EXAMPLE** **Jane** is on vacation in London. [*Jane* is the simple and complete subject.]

GO ON

EXERCISE B In each of the following sentences, underline the complete subject once. Then, underline the simple subject a second time. Hint: In some sentences, the simple subject and the complete subject will be the same.

Example 1. On a small leaf was a black-and-yellow caterpillar. [The sentence tells about the complete subject *a black-and-yellow caterpillar*. The simple subject is *caterpillar*.]

6. Jessica did her math homework on the porch of the house. [Who is the sentence about?]

7. A small flock of birds was flying north toward a lake.

8. Next to the vase is a beautifully framed picture of the family.

9. We are going to the Smoky Mountains on our next vacation.

10. Are the CDs from that record label still on sale?

The Compound Subject

1f. A *compound subject* consists of two or more subjects that are joined by a conjunction and that have the same verb.

A conjunction connects words or groups of words. The conjunctions that are usually used to connect the parts of a compound subject are *and* and *or*.

EXAMPLES **Sarah** and **Katie** are good soccer players. [The parts of the compound subject *Sarah* and *Katie* are joined by the conjunction *and*. They have the same verb, *are*.]

Patrick, Cindy, or **Chris** will bring the music. [The parts of the compound subject *Patrick, Cindy,* and *Chris* are joined by the conjunction *or*. They have the same verb, *will bring*.]

EXERCISE C In the following sentences, underline the parts of the compound subject. Then, circle the conjunction.

Example 1. Are Tom, Owen, (and) Jim going to the movies? [The conjunction is *and*. And connects the subjects *Tom, Owen,* and *Jim*.]

11. Books or folders are stacked next to the wall. [What is the sentence about? What connects the parts of the subject?]

12. The party supplies and the food will be picked up Saturday afternoon.

13. A grapefruit or an orange can be part of a good breakfast.

14. Wide rivers and narrow streams run through our home state.

15. Are Sally, Ted, and Bob sleeping yet?

HOLT HANDBOOK | First Course

The Predicate

The Simple Predicate

Sentences consist of two main parts: subjects and predicates.

1e. The *simple predicate* is the main word or word group that tells something about the subject. The simple predicate is also called the *verb.*

> **SIMPLE PREDICATE**   Many people **enjoy** the sound of crickets at night. [*Enjoy* is the simple predicate and tells what *people* do.]

> **REMINDER▶** A simple predicate can be a one-word verb or a verb phrase.

> **EXAMPLES**   Betsy **sprained** her ankle. [The verb is *sprained* and tells what Betsy did to her ankle.]
>
> **Are** the packages **arriving** today? [The verb phrase is *Are arriving.* The words in the verb phrase are separated by the complete subject *the packages* and tell what is happening to the packages.]

EXERCISE A Draw one line under the simple predicate in the following sentences.

Example 1. Sandra and Joe <u>are washing</u> the car. [The simple predicate *are washing* tells what Sandra and Joe are doing.]

1. My brother joined a chess team last year. [What did my brother do?]

2. We store boxes and other items in our attic.

3. In our basement you will find an old, dusty trunk.

4. Early Saturday morning, Pam, Lucy, and Cameron visited their grandparents.

5. A plant near the window fell to the floor unexpectedly.

The Complete Predicate

The *complete predicate* consists of all the words that describe the verb and complete its meaning.

> **COMPLETE PREDICATE**   Many people **enjoy the sound of crickets at night.** [The simple predicate is *enjoy.* The complete predicate is *enjoy the sound of crickets at night.*]

> **REMINDER▶** Sometimes the simple predicate is also the complete predicate.

> **EXAMPLE**   The dogs **are barking.** [*Are barking* is the simple predicate and the complete predicate.]

The predicate usually comes after the subject. Sometimes, however, part or all of the predicate comes before the subject.

> **EXAMPLES**   **On Monday** our science class **will visit the underground caverns.**
>
> **Swimming near the shore of the lake were** two beautiful ducks.

GO ON ▶

EXERCISE B Draw one line under the complete predicate in the following sentences. Then, draw a second line under the simple predicate.

Example 1. Does the dog <u>have enough water in its bowl</u>? [The complete predicate asks what the dog has. The simple predicate is *Does have*.]

6. The group of tourists visited the Metropolitan Museum of Art in New York. [What did the group of tourists do?]

7. Belinda is taking a class in ancient Egyptian art.

8. Traveling through Europe by train were some American students and their parents.

9. My aunt Barbara called us from Toronto last night.

10. Are the apples on the table?

The Compound Verb

1g. A *compound verb* is made up of two or more verbs that are joined by a conjunction and that have the same subject.

A conjunction connects words or groups of words. The conjunctions that are usually used to connect the parts of a compound verb are *and* and *or*.

> **EXAMPLE** The sparrows **hopped** around the yard and **chirped** brightly. [The compound verb is *hopped* and *chirped*. Both *hopped* and *chirped* tell about the same subject, *sparrows*. The compound verb is joined by the conjunction *and*.]

EXERCISE C Draw one line under the complete predicate in the following sentences. Then, draw a second line under the simple predicate. Be sure to underline each part of a compound verb and all parts of a verb phrase.

Example 1. Did the beetle <u>crawl into a hole and disappear</u>? [The complete predicate tells about the beetle. The simple predicate is the compound verb *did crawl* and *disappear*.]

11. At the beach we built sand castles and rode the waves. [What did we do? Where did we do it?]

12. At the ceremony he was given several awards.

13. Elaine borrowed my scarf yesterday and wore it to the concert.

14. On the weekend my cousin Jake usually skis or fishes.

15. Will the plans for the new house be finished by next week?

Classifying Sentences by Purpose

Every sentence has a purpose. All sentences can be classified as having one of these four purposes: *declarative*, *imperative*, *interrogative*, and *exclamatory*.

1h. | A *declarative sentence* makes a statement and ends with a period.

> **EXAMPLES** The store will close in ten minutes. [statement]
> Martin watched a film about dolphins. [statement]

1i. | An *imperative sentence* gives a command or makes a request. Most imperative sentences end with a period. A strong command ends with an exclamation point.

> **EXAMPLES** Study this painting by Picasso. [command]
> Please show me the photographs from your vacation. [request]

TIP Often, when people state a strong command, they speak more loudly than when they state a simple command or make a request. When you write, you can show this change in volume by using an exclamation point.

> **EXAMPLE** Don't step in the wet cement! [strong command]

NOTE The subject of a command or a request is always *you*. When *you* doesn't appear in the sentence, *you* is called the **understood subject**.

> **EXAMPLES** (You) Study this painting by Picasso. [command]
> (You) Please show me the photographs from your vacation. [request]
> (You) Don't step in the wet cement! [strong command]

The word *you* is the understood subject even when the person spoken to is addressed by name.

> **EXAMPLE** Louis, (you) please read the paragraph aloud. [In this request, *Louis* is used to get the listener's attention. *You*, not *Louis*, is the subject.]

EXERCISE A On the line provided, write *DEC* if the sentence is *declarative* or *IMP* if it is *imperative*.

Examples _DEC_ **1.** Gina lives near a city park. [This sentence expresses a statement.]

IMP **2.** Don't touch that hot soup kettle! [This sentence expresses a command.]

_____ **1.** Give your book report on Friday. [Does this sentence express a statement or a command?]

_____ **2.** Mario finished the race first. [Does this sentence express a statement or a command?]

_____ **3.** My great-grandfather came to the United States from Ireland.

_____ **4.** Last Saturday, Samantha and Rick rode their mountain bikes through the park.

_____ **5.** Check the water level!

_____ **6.** I think those are some parts from an old car.

_____ **7.** Please call me after school today.

GO ON

_____ **8.** Watch out for those wasps!

_____ **9.** Judy's older sister will one day be a veterinarian.

_____ **10.** Sandra, look at this warm, colorful scarf.

1j. An *interrogative sentence* asks a question and ends with a question mark.

  EXAMPLES Who wrote the poem about a raven? [question]
        Does this basketball need more air? [question]

1k. An *exclamatory sentence* shows excitement or expresses strong feeling and ends with an exclamation point.

  EXAMPLES My story won the contest! [exclamation]
        What a concert that was! [exclamation]

REMINDER A strong imperative may end with an exclamation mark.

  EXAMPLE Don't touch that! [strong command]

EXERCISE B Punctuate each of the following sentences with an appropriate end mark: a period, a question mark, or an exclamation point. Then, on the line provided, classify each sentence by writing *DEC* for *declarative*, *IMP* for *imperative*, *INT* for *interrogative*, or *EXC* for *exclamatory*.

Examples _IMP_ **1.** Tony, wait for me [This sentence expresses a command.]

     EXC **2.** What a great idea that is [This sentence expresses an exclamation.]

_____ **11.** Watch out for that car [Does this sentence express a command or a statement?]

_____ **12.** Did Anna meet your parents [Does this sentence express a strong emotion or a question?]

_____ **13.** What a hilarious joke that was

_____ **14.** Why did John go to the bookstore

_____ **15.** This is my brother's favorite book

_____ **16.** What a great time I'll have tonight

_____ **17.** Where is my new brown belt

_____ **18.** We will have turkey sandwiches for lunch

_____ **19.** Please turn the calendar page to the next month

_____ **20.** I can't believe we won

The Noun

Nouns

2a. A **noun** is a word or word group that is used to name a person, a place, a thing, or an idea.

PERSONS	Robert Frost, sister, governor, Dr. Muñoz
PLACES	classroom, Seattle, Carlsbad Caverns, store
THINGS	tree, desk, Statue of Liberty
IDEAS	honesty, envy, self-esteem, freedom

Did you notice that some nouns are made up of more than one word? A **compound noun** is a single noun made up of two or more words. The compound noun may be written as one word, as a hyphenated word, or as two or more words.

ONE WORD	bookcase, basketball, hourglass
HYPHENATED WORD	brother-in-law, great-uncle, warm-up
TWO WORDS	lieutenant governor, Miami Beach, parking lot

TIP To decide whether a word is a noun, try placing the word in the blank in one of the following sentences. If the word makes sense in the sentence, then the word is probably a noun.

EXAMPLES	I got a new _____.	*or*	I like _____.
	I got a new <u>computer</u>.		I like <u>honesty</u>.

EXERCISE A Underline each noun in the sentences below. Hint: Remember to underline all parts of a compound noun.

Examples 1. <u>Brandon</u> and his <u>stepfather</u> live in <u>Colorado Springs</u>. [*Brandon* and *stepfather* name people. *Colorado Springs* names a place.]

2. This <u>city</u> in <u>Colorado</u> is near <u>Pike National Forest</u>. [*City* names a thing. *Colorado* and *Pike National Forest* name places.]

1. Pikes Peak is a high mountaintop in the Rocky Mountains. [Which words name places or things?]

2. This range of mountains lies to the west of Colorado Springs. [Which words name places or things?]

3. Many people enjoy the view from Pikes Peak, which is 14,110 feet in height.

4. Brandon and his great-grandfather often drive through the countryside.

5. These trips give the two men great happiness.

6. Wild animals such as elk and marmots live in the mountains.

7. Marmots are small, furry animals that have small ears, a short tail, and strong claws.

8. Many small rodents, such as chipmunks, can be very cute.

GO ON

9. However, forest rangers warn hikers that wild animals can carry diseases.

10. Visitors must not give food to the wildlife or touch the animals.

Common Nouns and Proper Nouns

You may have noticed that some nouns are capitalized and others are not. A *common noun* names any one of a group of persons, places, things, or ideas. A common noun is generally not capitalized. A *proper noun* names a particular person, place, thing, or idea. A proper noun begins with a capital letter. Proper nouns are often made up of more than one word.

> **COMMON NOUNS**   poet, state, book, religion
> **PROPER NOUNS**   Emily Dickinson, North Carolina, *Number the Stars*, Islam

TIP To identify a proper noun, try placing *a* or *an* in front of the noun. If *a* or *an* does not make sense in front of the noun, the noun is probably a proper noun. For example, *a Mount Rushmore* doesn't make sense. Therefore, *Mount Rushmore* is a proper noun.

EXERCISE B Identify each of the following nouns as a common noun or a proper noun. On the line provided, write *C* for *common noun* or *P* for *proper noun*.

Examples __C__ **1.** guitar [*Guitar* names a general thing and is not capitalized.]

__P__ **2.** Central Park [*Central Park* names a specific place and is capitalized.]

_____**11.** *Summer of the Monkeys* [specific thing or not a specific thing?]

_____**12.** friend [specific person or not a specific person?]

_____**13.** Coretta Scott King

_____**14.** ex-president

_____**15.** notebook

_____**16.** Civil War

_____**17.** high school

_____**18.** Canada

_____**19.** Golden Gate Bridge

_____**20.** song

_____**21.** swarm

_____**22.** wasp

_____**23.** "John Henry"

_____**24.** Emily Dickinson

_____**25.** Ms. Valdez

_____**26.** dentist

_____**27.** "The Stone"

_____**28.** kitten

_____**29.** cow

_____**30.** Smokey

Pronouns and Antecedents

The Pronoun

2b. A *pronoun* is a word that is used in place of one or more nouns or pronouns.

We often use pronouns to avoid repeating a name or a word many times in a row.

EXAMPLES Did Ken say Ken found Ken's coat?

Did Ken say **he** found **his** coat? [The pronouns *he* and *his* replace *Ken* and *Ken's*.]

The singers warmed up the singers' voices until the teacher joined the singers.

The singers warmed up **their** voices until the teacher joined **them.** [The pronouns *their* and *them* replace *singers'* and *singers*.]

Someone left someone's library card in this book.

Someone left **his or her** library card in this book. [The compound pronoun *his* or *her* replaces *someone's*.]

EXERCISE A Underline each pronoun in the following sentences. Some sentences have more than one pronoun.

Examples 1. Did Lorenzo say how <u>he</u> broke <u>his</u> arm? [*He* and *his* are used in order not to repeat *Lorenzo*.]

2. The hamster ran on <u>its</u> exercise wheel. [*Its* is used in order not to repeat *hamster*.]

1. Rob noticed a friendly dog behind him. [Which word is used in place of *Rob*?]

2. The volleyball player enjoyed a cool drink of water after her game. [Which word is used in place of *player*?]

3. The castle had a deep moat at its base.

4. We discussed our weekend plans.

5. Eddie and Marisa carried snacks and water with them.

6. Linda asked her to help with the party arrangements.

7. Nick and Jake helped themselves to the delicious dinner.

8. The police officers always have their radios with them.

9. Students, did you write your name at the top of the test?

10. Mr. Raskin said, "I enjoy the discussions with my students."

`GO ON ➡`

The Antecedent

The word or word group that a pronoun stands for (or refers to) is called its *antecedent*.

TIP To find the antecedent, ask yourself *who* or *what* the pronoun stands for.

> *antecedent*   *pronoun pronoun*
> **EXAMPLES** **Antonio,** where did **you** get **your** skateboard? [The pronouns *you* and *your*
>
> stand for *Antonio* and *Antonio's.*]
>
> *antecedent*   *pronoun*
> The **dog** is shedding **its** fur all over the furniture. [The pronoun *its* stands
>
> for *dog's.*]

Sometimes the antecedent is not stated. Here are some reasons why you might not use an antecedent.

- You might not use an antecedent when you are talking or writing about yourself or when you are talking or writing to someone in particular. The audience already knows who you are and who they are.

> **EXAMPLE** **I'll** join **you** for a swim in the lake. [*I* refers to the speaker, and *you* refers to the person spoken to.]

- Sometimes, you don't know what the antecedent is, such as when you ask a question.

> **EXAMPLE** **Who** sent you that postcard? [The speaker doesn't know who *who* is.]

- Indefinite pronouns such as *someone, everybody,* and *many* are often used without antecedents.

> **EXAMPLE** **Everyone** enjoyed art class today. [The indefinite pronoun *Everyone* does not have an antecedent.]

EXERCISE B Draw an arrow from the underlined pronoun to its antecedent in each of the following sentences. If the antecedent is not stated, write *none* on the line provided.

Example _____ **1.** Did Joyce say when she earned her black belt? [*She* stands for *Joyce.*]

_____ **11.** The goldfish quickly ate its food. [What does *its* stand for?]

_____ **12.** The firefighters put away their equipment. [What does *their* stand for?]

_____ **13.** Would you help me with dinner tonight?

_____ **14.** Maureen said, "I teach an aerobics class each Tuesday evening."

_____ **15.** Jason, the poem you wrote has wonderful imagery!

Personal Pronouns, Reflexive and Intensive Pronouns, Demonstrative Pronouns, Interrogative Pronouns

Personal Pronouns

A *personal pronoun* refers to the person speaking (*first person*), the person spoken to (*second person*), or the person spoken about (*third person*).

FIRST PERSON	I will work hard on the project. [The personal pronoun *I* refers to the person speaking.]
SECOND PERSON	Are **you** going to the music festival? [The personal pronoun *you* refers to the person to whom someone is speaking.]
THIRD PERSON	**He** travels often with **his** sister to South America. [The personal pronouns *He* and *his* refer to the person about whom someone is speaking.]

EXERCISE A Underline the personal pronouns in each of the following sentences.

Example 1. I enjoy weekend activities with my family. [*I* and *my* refer to the person speaking.]

1. My sister usually bakes something delicious. [Which word is a personal pronoun?]

2. She sometimes invites friends over to our house.

3. Our parents sometimes take us to the movies.

4. They plan something different to do every weekend.

5. What do you do in your free time?

Reflexive and Intensive Pronouns

A *reflexive pronoun* refers to the subject. It is necessary to the meaning of the sentence. An *intensive pronoun* emphasizes a noun or a pronoun. It is not necessary to the meaning of the sentence. All reflexive and intensive pronouns end in *–self* or *–selves*.

REFLEXIVE PRONOUN	Morgan treated **herself** to a fruit smoothie. [*Herself* refers to the subject, *Morgan.*]
INTENSIVE PRONOUN	The awards were sent directly to the winners **themselves.** [*Themselves* emphasizes *winners.*]

TIP▶ If you're not sure whether a pronoun is reflexive or intensive, use this test: Read the sentence aloud, leaving out the pronoun. Ask yourself whether the basic meaning of the sentence stayed the same. If the meaning stayed the same, the pronoun is intensive. If the meaning changed, the pronoun is reflexive.

EXAMPLES	I enjoyed **myself** at the game. [*Myself* refers to *I.* Without *myself*, the sentence doesn't make sense. The pronoun is reflexive.]
	Elsa made breakfast **herself.** [*Herself* emphasizes *Elsa.* Without *herself*, the meaning stays the same. The pronoun is intensive.]

EXERCISE B Identify the underlined pronoun in each of the following sentences. Write on the line provided *REF* for *reflexive* or *INT* for *intensive*.

Example _INT_ **1.** He prepared a study guide <u>himself</u>. [*Himself* can be left out. It is not

necessary for the meaning of the sentence.]

_____ **6.** They devoted <u>themselves</u> to the study of Brazil. [Is the pronoun necessary?]

_____ **7.** Ms. Nelson <u>herself</u> had been to Brazil during her vacation.

_____ **8.** Dan prepared <u>himself</u> well for his speech on products of Brazil.

_____ **9.** In fact, Brazil <u>itself</u> is the world's fifth largest country.

_____ **10.** Brazilians have devoted <u>themselves</u> to good education in their country.

Demonstrative Pronouns

A *demonstrative pronoun* points out a person, a place, a thing, or an idea.

> **EXAMPLES** **This** is a fantastic book about giraffes. [*This* points out *book*.]
>
> Are **these** your cousins from Nebraska? [*These* points out *cousins*.]

Interrogative Pronouns

An *interrogative pronoun* introduces a question. The interrogative pronouns are *what*, *which*, *who*, *whom*, and *whose*.

> **EXAMPLES** **Who** will bring the party favors?
>
> **What** is your favorite color?

EXERCISE C Identify each underlined pronoun by writing on the line provided *DEM* for *demonstrative* or *INTER* for *interrogative*.

Example _INTER_ **1.** To <u>whom</u> did Linda lend the book about rain forests? [*Whom* introduces a

question.]

_____ **11.** <u>Who</u> knows where rain forests are located? [Does the pronoun introduce a question or

point out something?]

_____ **12.** <u>These</u> are forests in the hot, wet climates near the equator.

_____ **13.** <u>Whose</u> map shows the equator?

_____ **14.** <u>That</u> is an imaginary circle around the earth.

_____ **15.** <u>What</u> are the continents near the equator?

HOLT HANDBOOK | First Course

Indefinite and Relative Pronouns

Indefinite Pronouns

Personal pronouns refer to specific people, places, things, or ideas. An **indefinite pronoun** refers to a person, place, thing, or idea that may or may not be specifically named. Some common indefinite pronouns are *all, both, none, other, any, everything, no one,* and *one.*

> **EXAMPLES** Does **anyone** know the answer? [The indefinite pronoun *anyone* does not refer to a specific person.]
>
> We have **everything** we need for the picnic. [The indefinite pronoun *everything* does not refer to a specific thing.]

EXERCISE A Underline the indefinite pronoun in each of the following sentences.

Examples 1. I loaned my pencil sharpener to <u>somebody</u> yesterday. [*Somebody* does not refer to a specific person.]

2. <u>No one</u> saw the horsefly until after it had already bitten Alan. [*No one* does not refer to a specific person.]

1. Nervousness came over many of the newscasters just before they went on camera. [Which word does not refer to someone or something specific?]

2. Both of the women were thrilled when they passed the difficult tests and became firefighters. [Which word does not refer to someone or something specific?]

3. I will be happy if either of the sprinters from Anderson High School wins the race.

4. All of the faces on Mount Rushmore were carved into a granite cliff.

5. For the last six months, several of the club members have been saving money.

6. One of the players hit a home run in the first inning.

7. The German shepherd at the animal shelter will be adopted by someone very soon.

8. Few of the lessons did not make sense on the first day of class.

9. Asteroids that smashed into the moon probably formed some of the moon's craters.

10. Moths can live in nearly all of the parts of the world, including in jungles and on ice caps.

Relative Pronouns

A *relative pronoun* introduces a subordinate clause. The subordinate clause adds information about the noun that comes before it. Common relative pronouns are *that, which, who, whom,* and *whose.*

> **EXAMPLES** This is the shirt **that I bought yesterday**. [The relative pronoun *that* introduces the subordinate clause *that I bought yesterday*. The subordinate clause adds information about *shirt*.]

GO ON

The number on Dora's jersey is eight, **which is her favorite number.** [The relative pronoun *which* introduces the subordinate clause *which is her favorite number.* The subordinate clause adds information about *eight.*]

The person **whose number is called** should come to the front of the room. [The relative pronoun *whose* introduces the subordinate clause *whose number is called.* The subordinate clause adds information about *person.*]

NOTE *Which, who, whom,* and *whose* can also be used as interrogative pronouns.

RELATIVE PRONOUN The girl **who** just entered the school sings in the chorus. [*Who* introduces the relative clause *who just entered the school.*]

INTERROGATIVE PRONOUN **Who** else sings in the chorus? [*Who* introduces a question.]

EXERCISE B The subordinate clause is underlined in each sentence below. Circle the relative pronoun in each clause.

Examples 1. My aunt, (whose) name is Kendra, is a marine biologist. [*Whose* introduces the subordinate clause.]

2. The teddy bear (that) no longer has a nose is the baby's favorite. [*That* introduces the subordinate clause.]

11. Please hand me the pen that fell on the floor. [Which word introduces the subordinate clause?]

12. Mr. Oliver is a teacher who tells funny stories during class. [Which word introduces the subordinate clause?]

13. The actor whose picture is on this poster played in a celebrity golf tournament last weekend.

14. My friend has a long middle name that is hard to remember.

15. The photograph that is on the magazine cover makes me want to go swimming.

16. Mount Hood, which is an inactive volcano, has the highest peak in Oregon.

17. New Zealand is a country that has hundreds of waterfalls.

18. Georgia's son, who was born last May, likes to make silly faces.

19. Jesse Owens, who was a U.S. track-and-field star, won four gold medals at the 1936 Summer Olympic Games.

20. During the Chinese New Year, which lasts four days, people dress in colorful dragon costumes.

Adjectives and Articles

The Adjective

2c. An *adjective* is a word that is used to modify a noun or a pronoun.

A noun or pronoun names a person, place, thing, or idea.

To *modify* a word means to describe the word or to make its meaning more definite. An adjective modifies a noun or a pronoun by telling *what kind, which one, how much,* or *how many.*

WHAT KIND?	**German** pen pal, **happy** dog, **green** grass
WHICH ONE OR ONES?	**third** bus stop, **those** lockers, **every** desk
HOW MUCH? OR HOW MANY?	**some** fruit, **four** quarters, **no** shoes

Sometimes an adjectives comes after the word it modifies.

EXAMPLES The kitten, **energetic** and **playful,** chased a butterfly. [The adjectives *energetic* and *playful* describe *kitten.*]

The butterfly is **yellow.** [The predicate adjective *yellow* describes *butterfly.*]

NOTE Remember that proper adjectives, such as *German* and *Canadian*, are capitalized.

EXERCISE A Underline each adjective in each of the following sentences. Some sentences may contain more than one adjective. Do not underline *a, an,* or *the* in this exercise.

Examples 1. The story, short and suspenseful, entertained me. [*Short* and *suspenseful* describe *story.*]

2. Some students enrolled in the French class. [*Some* describes *students. French* describes *class.*]

1. In the box lay beautiful gems. [Which word describes *gems*?]

2. The clean table was shiny. [Which words describe *table*?]

3. Shelby lent ten dollars to a good friend.

4. That frog lives in a small pond.

5. A new student has joined the seventh grade.

6. The artist, creative and successful, opened a gallery.

7. Few people have climbed to the top of the icy mountain.

8. A piece of African art was hanging above the large fireplace.

9. The enthusiastic audience applauded each act of the play.

10. No points were scored until several minutes had passed.

GO ON

Articles

The adjectives *a, an,* and *the* are called **articles.** *A* and *an* are called *indefinite articles* because they refer to any member of a general group.

- *A* is used before a word beginning with a consonant sound.
- *An* is used before a word beginning with a vowel sound.

> **EXAMPLES** **A** mosquito bit me. [*Mosquito* begins with a consonant sound.]
>
> **An** umbrella shields you from a rain shower. [*Umbrella* begins with a vowel sound.]
>
> The circus clown rode **a** unicycle. [Even though *u* is a vowel, the word *unicycle* begins with a consonant sound. Do you hear the *y* sound?]
>
> I'll meet you in **an** hour. [Even though *h* is a consonant, the word *hour* begins with a vowel sound. The *h* is not pronounced.]

The is called the *definite article* because it refers to someone or something in particular.

> **EXAMPLES** **The** mosquito bit me. [A specific mosquito bit me.]
>
> May I borrow **the** umbrella? [I want to borrow a specific umbrella.]

EXERCISE B Underline all of the articles in the following sentences. Some sentences may have more than one article.

Examples 1. Could you pass me an envelope and a pen? [*An envelope* refers to any envelope.

  A pen refers to any pen.]

2. I pulled the book from my backpack. [*The book* refers to a specific book.]

11. Megan found the bracelet under her desk. [Which word makes *bracelet* specific?]

12. Philip sketched a motorcycle on his notebook. [Which word makes *motorcycle* not specific?]

13. A light bulb in the kitchen has burned out.

14. There is an owl on the top branch of that tree.

15. I offered the cold fruit juice to my friend.

16. The treasure map had an *X* drawn on it in black ink.

17. My entry in the contest received an honorable mention.

18. I sing in a choir in my church.

19. Janice sliced a banana into the bowl of cereal.

20. Our hotel room was on an upper floor.

The Verb

What Is a Verb?

3a.	A *verb* is a word that tells the action or a state of being.

EXAMPLES   Jesse **ran** around the house three times. [The verb *ran* tells what action Jesse performed.]

After that, Jesse **was** very thirsty. [The verb *was* does not tell about an action. Instead, it tells something about Jesse's state of being.]

EXERCISE A   Underline the verb in each of the following sentences.

Examples 1. The moon <u>is</u> the earth's closest neighbor. [The verb *is* tells something about the moon's state of being.]

2. It <u>reflects</u> light from the sun. [The verb *reflects* tells what action *It* performs.]

1. The moon orbits the earth. [Which word tells what action the *moon* performs?]

2. It is about one quarter the size of earth. [Which word tells something about the state of being of *It*?]

3. Humans first landed on the moon in 1969.

4. The astronauts left footprints in the fine dust.

5. Meteors crushed rocks into dust.

6. The moon has no atmosphere.

7. Impressions from meteors and footprints last for a long time.

8. Many of the moon's features are visible to the eye.

9. One side of the moon never faces earth.

10. Sometimes, the moon blocks the light of the sun from the earth.

Helping Verbs and Main Verbs

The main verb is the word that shows the action or state of being in a sentence. Sometimes, other verbs are added to the main verb to make the main verb more specific. These other verbs are called *helping verbs. Helping verbs* are sometimes called *auxiliary verbs.*

3d.	A *helping verb* helps the main verb express an action or a state of being.

Some common helping verbs include *am, is, was, were, do, have, can, must,* and *will.*

EXAMPLES   Monica **will** be at third base. [The helping verb *will* helps the main verb *be* express a future state of being.]

The lilac **should have** bloomed by now. [The helping verbs *should* and *have* help the main verb *bloomed* express an expected action.]

GO ON ▶

A *verb phrase* contains at least one main verb and one or more helping verbs.

VERB PHRASES A round of applause **was given** to the award-winning teacher. [The helping verb is *was* and the main verb is *given*.]

My dog Pepper **has** not yet **found** her missing toy. [The helping verb is *has* and the main verb is *found*. The words *not* and *yet* are adverbs.]

Have three more dogs **been adopted** from the shelter today? [The helping verbs *Have* and *been* help the main verb *adopted* express the action that occurred in the past. Notice that helping verbs are sometimes separated from the main verb by other parts of the sentence.]

EXERCISE B Underline the verb phrase in each of the following sentences. Then, draw a second line under each helping verb.

Examples 1. All eight birds had been eating from the feeder. [The word that shows the action of the sentence is *eating, so eating* is the main verb. The other verbs, *had* and *been,* are helping verbs.]

 2. Did Tracey win a blue ribbon? [The word that shows the action of the sentence is *win,* so *win* is the main verb. The other verb in the sentence, *Did,* is a helping verb.]

11. Thomas is leading the overall competition. [Which word shows the action? What other verb is helping it?]

12. The radio station has played that song three times today. [Which word shows the action? What other verb is helping it?]

13. Those rules may be out of date.

14. Have you heard the weather forecast?

15. This scarecrow should protect the garden.

16. The kitten has been growing very quickly.

17. Today's classes have not been canceled.

18. Would that piece have completed the puzzle?

19. A chipmunk has been making tunnels under this field.

20. When will Sarah be visiting her cousins?

Action Verbs and Linking Verbs

Action Verbs

Verbs can be identified as action verbs or as linking verbs.

3b.   An *action verb* is a verb that shows action.

>   **EXAMPLES**   Sharon **cooked** tonight's dinner. [The verb *cooked* shows physical action.]
>   I **understand** your concern. [The verb *understand* shows mental action.]

REMINDER When you identify action verbs, remember to include any helping verbs.

>   **EXAMPLES**   Who **should be considered** the best baseball player in history? [The main
>   verb is *considered* and the helping verbs are *should* and *be*. The verb
>   phrase *should be considered* shows mental action.]
>   **Will** the geese **fly** south for the winter soon? [The helping verb *Will* is
>   separated from the main verb *fly*. The verb phrase *Will fly* shows
>   physical action.]

EXERCISE A Underline the action verbs in each of the following sentences. Remember to include any
helping verbs. Hint: Helping verbs are verbs that are added to the main verb to make the main verb
more specific.

Examples 1. Victor runs four miles in the park several times a week. [*Runs* tells what action *Victor*

performs.]

2. Does anyone want more water? [*Does want* tells what action *anyone* performs.]

1. Karen sent an e-mail to her brother. [Which word tells the action *Karen* performs?]

2. Have you found the receipt? [Which words tells the action *you* perform?]

3. Mr. Sullivan will be teaching Spanish next year.

4. How long have you known about this book?

5. David forgave me at once.

6. A picture of an animal had been drawn on the wall of the cave.

7. The Wildcats lost the game last night.

8. Can you read this handwriting?

9. Answer the third question, please.

10. I barely remember my third birthday.

GO ON

Linking Verbs

3c. A *linking verb* is a verb that expresses a state of being. A linking verb connects, or links, the subject to a word or word group that identifies or describes the subject.

Many linking verbs are forms of the verb *be*.

is	are	was	will be
am	has been	were	

Other common linking verbs include the following:

appear	feel	sound
become	seem	taste

EXAMPLES The new class president **is** Josie Franklin. [The linking verb *is* connects the subject, *president*, to the word group, *Josie Franklin*, that identifies it.]

Was the baby raccoon **feeling** better? [The linking verb *Was feeling* connects the subject, *raccoon*, to the word, *better*, that describes it.]

EXERCISE B Underline the linking verbs in each of the following sentences. Remember to include any helping verbs. Hint: Helping verbs are verbs that are added to the main verb to make the main verb more specific.

Examples 1. Is the woman in the green dress the guest speaker? [The linking verb *Is* links *woman* to *speaker*.]

2. Mark has been feeling more confident lately. [The main verb is *feeling*, and the helping verbs are *has* and *been*. The linking verb *has been feeling* links *Mark* to *confident*.]

11. That might be your longest jump yet! [Which words link *That* to *jump*?]

12. This yogurt tastes wonderful. [Which word links *yogurt* to *wonderful*?]

13. Suddenly, the sky became cloudy.

14. Were you the one in the red hat?

15. Cats can be sneaky.

16. In the yard, the leaves are in a pile.

17. The choir sounds beautiful tonight.

18. Mary had been treasurer for the past two years.

19. How does water become snow?

20. Michelle felt sad about the end of the school year.

The Adverb

What Is an Adverb?

3g. An *adverb* is a word that modifies a verb, an adjective, or another adverb.

REMINDER▶ A *verb* is a word or word group that shows action or state of being. Some examples of verbs include *leave, wash, walk,* and *be.* An **adjective** is a word that modifies or describes a noun or a pronoun. Some examples of adjectives include *full, unusual,* and *simple.*

Adverbs answer the following questions: Where? How often? How long? When? To what extent? How much? How?

EXAMPLES Leave the grapes **here,** and I will wash them **soon.** [The adverb *here* modifies the verb *Leave* and tells *where.* The adverb *soon* modifies the verb phrase *will wash* and tells *when.*]

I walked **extremely carefully** on the ice. [The adverb *extremely* modifies the adverb *carefully* and tells *to what extent.* The adverb *carefully* modifies the verb *walked* and tells *how.*]

Was the bucket **completely** full? [The adverb *completely* modifies the adjective *full* and tells *how much.*]

We will be friends **forever** and will visit **frequently.** [The adverb *forever* modifies the verb phrase *will be* and tells *how long.* The adverb *frequently* modifies the verb phrase *will visit* and tells *how often.*]

EXERCISE A Draw an arrow from the underlined adverb in each of the following sentences to the word or words it modifies. Hint: An adverb modifies each word in a verb phrase, not just the main verb.

Example 1. Paul hasn't discovered any new stars yet, but he is trying. [The adverb *n't (not)* modifies the verb *has discovered* by telling *to what extent.*]

1. Paul will eventually become a scientist. [*Eventually* tells *when* about which words?]

2. He continuously observes the world.

3. Sometimes he studies the stars and the planets.

4. He reads books about very unusual plants and animals.

5. He is almost never absent from science class at school.

The Position of Adverbs

Adverbs may appear at various places in a sentence. Adverbs may come before, after, or between the words they modify.

EXAMPLES I **soon** realized my mistake. [The adverb *soon* modifies the verb *realized*.]

I realized my mistake **soon.**

Soon I realized my mistake.

I had **soon** realized my mistake. [The adverb *soon* modifies the verb phrase *had realized*.]

EXERCISE B Draw one line under the adverb in the following sentences. Then, draw an arrow to the word or words the adverb modifies. Remember to draw the arrow to each part of a verb phrase. Hint: Each sentence has only one adverb.

Examples 1. We had been secretly planning the party for weeks. [The adverb *secretly* describes the verb phrase *had been planning* by telling *how*.]

2. Of course, we didn't tell Cindy anything about it. [The adverb *n't (not)* describes the verb *did tell* by telling *to what extent*.]

6. Cindy had already turned thirteen. [Which word modifies the verb *had turned*?]

7. Her birthday was celebrated by her family in a very simple way. [Which word modifies the adjective *simple*?]

8. Quietly, her friends were planning a big surprise party.

9. We would celebrate her birthday late!

10. She would never suspect this surprise party.

11. When would the day of the party arrive?

12. All of Cindy's friends eagerly gathered at my house.

13. I called Cindy and casually invited her to my house.

14. She came immediately and knocked on the door.

15. I opened the door, and all of us happily shouted, "Happy birthday!"

The Preposition

3h. A *preposition* is a word that shows the relationship of a noun or pronoun to another word.

EXAMPLES The helicopter flew **above** the mountains. [The preposition *above* shows the relationship of *mountains* to *flew*.]

The rug **near** you needs cleaning. [The preposition *near* shows the relationship of *you* to *rug*.]

By using a different preposition, you can change the relationship of *mountains* to *flew* and of *you* to *rug*.

EXAMPLES The helicopter flew **behind** the mountains.

The rug **underneath** you needs cleaning.

Commonly Used Prepositions

about	before	for	out	unlike
above	behind	from	over	until
across	below	in	past	up
after	beneath	inside	since	upon
against	between	into	through	with
along	beyond	like	throughout	within
among	by	near	to	without
around	down	of	toward	
as	during	off	under	
at	except	on	underneath	

EXERCISE A Underline the prepositions in each of the following sentences. Hint: Some sentences have more than one preposition.

Examples 1. During the break, Felicity rested her head upon her arms. [The preposition *During* shows the relationship between *rested* and *break*. The preposition *upon* shows the relationship between *head* and *arms*.]

2. Clint looked for the healthiest puppy of the litter. [The preposition *for* shows the relationship between *looked* and *puppy*. The preposition *of* shows the relationship between *puppy* and *litter*.]

1. Are gloves and hats on sale this week? [Which word shows the relationship between *Are* and *sale*?]

2. Tommy's parents will serve as chaperones during the dance. [Which word shows the relationship between *serve* and *chaperones*? Which word shows the relationship between *serve* and *dance*?]

3. Saturday is the busiest day of the week for our family.

4. We rested underneath the huge branches of a shady tree.

5. The dump truck rumbled into the construction site.

6. Noises from another classroom came through the walls.

7. Everyone except Erik returned to the sideline.

8. I have not felt well since yesterday.

9. The raccoon scampered across the yard and disappeared into the hedge.

10. Diane saw a dragonfly outside the window.

A preposition may be made up of more than one word. Such a preposition is called a *compound preposition.*

EXAMPLE Jimmy walked **in front of** Susan. [The preposition *in front of* shows the relationship of *walked* to *Susan.*]

Commonly Used Compound Prepositions

in front of	instead of	next to	out of	up to

EXERCISE B Underline the preposition(s) in each of the following sentences. Remember to underline all words in a compound preposition. Hint: Some sentences have more than one preposition.

Examples 1. Instead of the leather coat, I bought the wool sweater. [The words *instead of* show the relationship between *bought* and *coat.*]

      2. Gwyneth sits next to Jamal in science class. [The words *next to* show the relationship between *sits* and *Jamal.* The word *in* shows the relationship between *sits* and *class.*]

11. In front of the building, a delivery truck was parked. [Which words show the relationship between *was parked* and *building*?]

12. Alex, you may spend up to ten dollars on the gift. [Which words show the relationship between *may spend* and *dollars*? Which word shows the relationship between *may spend* and *gift*?]

13. The kitten batted the ball under the sofa.

14. The guests helped themselves to the celery on the plate.

15. Will you bring me the scissors when you finish with them?

16. The students filed out of the classroom when they heard the fire alarm.

17. The next meeting will be at our house.

18. Place the lamp near the chair but not next to it.

19. Instead of beef, Morty put spicy chicken in the enchiladas.

20. The pancakes were taken out of the pan and placed on a platter.

Conjunctions and Interjections

Coordinating Conjunctions

3i. A *conjunction* is a word that joins words or word groups.

> **EXAMPLES** They have planted trees, shrubs, bushes, **and** flowers in the backyard. [The conjunction *and* joins the words *trees, shrubs, bushes,* and *flowers.*]
>
> **Either** you must put your costume on now, **or** you will be late for your entrance. [The conjunctions *Either* and *or* join the clauses *you must put your costume on now* and *you will be late for your entrance.*]

Coordinating conjunctions join words to words, phrases to phrases, and clauses to clauses.

The coordinating conjunctions are *and, but, for, nor, or, so,* and *yet.*

> **EXAMPLES** Eric **or** David [The conjunction *or* joins two words.]
>
> in the air **and** on the ground [The conjunction *and* joins the two phrases *in the air* and *on the ground.*]
>
> We played our best, **but** we lost to a better team. [The conjunction *but* joins the two clauses *We played our best* and *we lost to a better team.*]

EXERCISE A Underline the coordinating conjunction in each of the following sentences.

Example 1. The restaurant was closed, <u>so</u> they made sandwiches instead. [The conjunction *so* joins the two clauses *The restaurant was closed* and *they made sandwiches instead.*]

1. I have soccer practice on Monday, Wednesday, and Friday afternoons. [Which word joins the nouns *Monday, Wednesday,* and *Friday*?]

2. He said that all of the baseballs or bats have been returned to the store.

3. The cat did not run away, nor did it come closer.

4. We wanted to watch the parade, but we couldn't see over the crowd.

5. Find some books on that subject, for your research is due Monday.

Correlative Conjunctions

Correlative conjunctions are pairs of conjunctions. The pairs work together to join words to words, phrases to phrases, and clauses to clauses.

The correlative conjunctions are

both . . . and	not only . . . but also	either . . . or
whether . . . or	neither . . . nor	

> **EXAMPLE** **Not only** did I finish the book, **but** I **also** wrote my report. [The pair of conjunctions joins the two clauses *did I finish the book* and *I wrote my report.*]

EXERCISE B Underline the correlative conjunctions in each of the following sentences.

Example 1. <u>Either</u> I can make macaroni for dinner, <u>or</u> I can serve salad. [The conjunction

Either…or joins the clauses *I can make macaroni* and *I can serve salad.*]

6. Neither Alice nor Paula expected the cats to get along. [Which words join the words *Alice* and

Paula?]

7. Dad isn't sure whether William Safire or Ellen Goodman is his favorite journalist.

8. My sister will take either Spanish or French next semester.

9. That type of grass not only prevents erosion but also requires little water.

10. We have seen both sparrows and cardinals at the birdbath.

Interjections

| **3j.** | An *interjection* is a word that expresses emotion. |

An interjection can be left out of a sentence without changing the meaning of the sentence. Commonly used interjections include *aha, ouch, wow, oh, yikes, hurray, oops, well,* and *yippee.*

Interjections that express strong emotion are followed by an exclamation point.

> **EXAMPLES**   **Yikes!** You scared me!
>
> What a great ending! **Wow!**

Interjections that express mild emotion are separated from the rest of the sentence by a comma.

> **EXAMPLES**   **Well,** I guess we will have to start again.
>
> That tree is, **oh,** about three hundred years old. [Notice that an interjection in the middle of a sentence is set off by two commas.]

EXERCISE C Underline the interjection in each of the following sentences.

Example 1. <u>Wow</u>! There's no telling how much Marsha's cat weighs. [The interjection *Wow*

expresses a strong emotion.]

11. Whew! You finished the exam twenty minutes early! [Which word expresses a strong emotion?]

12. We could have eaten the leftover lasagna, but, well, I think my brother got to it first.

13. Oops! I meant to go the other way.

14. Our team won the state championship! Hurray!

15. I would like to introduce you to her, but, oh, I don't know where she went.

Recognizing Complements

Every sentence has a subject and a verb. Many sentences have other words that complete the meaning of the verb. These words are called *complements*.

4a. A *complement* is a word or word group that completes the meaning of a verb.

                    S   V   C
EXAMPLES Tom Sawyer painted the **fence.** [The complement *fence* completes the

meaning of the verb *painted*.]
                  S   V   C
The title of the book is ***The Adventures of Tom Sawyer.*** [The complement

The Adventures of Tom Sawyer completes the meaning of the verb *is*.]
                  S   V   C
This flower smells **wonderful.** [The complement *wonderful* completes the

meaning of the verb *smells*.]

EXERCISE A In each of the following sentences, draw an arrow from the underlined complement to the verb whose meaning it completes.

Example 1. Are the birds on the pond <u>swans</u>? [The complement *swans* completes the meaning of

the verb *Are*.]

1. Thea kicked the soccer <u>ball</u>. [Which word is completed by *ball*?]

2. The tomato soup smells <u>delicious</u>.

3. Our guests are <u>they</u>.

4. The water felt <u>warm</u>.

5. Katrina placed a <u>bookmark</u> in her book.

TIP To recognize a complement, use this test. Ask yourself the question *what* (or *whom*)? after the subject and the verb. The word that answers the question *what* is probably a complement.
                    S   V   C
          EXAMPLE My sister sang a **song.** [My sister sang a *what*? She sang a song, so *song* is the complement.]

When you are looking for complements, it helps to know where *not* to look.

• An adverb is never a complement. As you may remember, an *adverb* is a word that describes a verb. Many adverbs end in *–ly*.

          ADVERB Dena read **quickly.** [The adverb *quickly* describes the verb *read* by telling *how* Dena read.]

          COMPLEMENT Dena read that **book.** [The complement *book* completes the meaning of the verb *read*. The complement tells *what* Dena read.]

GO ON ➡

Developmental Language Skills

- A complement is never in a prepositional phrase. A *prepositional phrase* begins with a preposition, ends with an object of a preposition, and includes the words in between. Common prepositions are *at, for, from, in, of, on, near, to,* and *under.*

PREPOSITIONAL PHRASE	Shelly is singing **in the car.** [The prepositional phrase *in the car* is an adverb phrase. It tells *where* Shelly is singing.]
COMPLEMENT	Shelly is driving the **car.** [The complement *car* is a noun. It tells *what* Shelly is driving.]

EXERCISE B Underline the complement in each of the following sentences. If the sentence has no complement, write *none* on the line provided. Hint: You may first want to cross out any adverbs or prepositional phrases in each sentence.

Examples _____ **1.** Susan visited her grandmother in Alaska. [*Grandmother* answers the question *Susan visited whom? Grandmother* is the complement. *In Alaska* cannot include a complement because it is a prepositional phrase.]

_____ **2.** Is the box on the table quite heavy? [*Heavy* answers the question *Is the box what? On the table* cannot include a complement because it is a prepositional phrase.]

_____ **6.** Carlos hung a poster on the wall. [Which word answers the question *Carlos hung what?*]

_____ **7.** I wrote a note to myself. [Which word answers the question *I wrote what?*]

_____ **8.** We welcome you to our home.

_____ **9.** Did Earl complete the entire puzzle by himself?

_____ **10.** Those drums sound too loud!

_____ **11.** The sand felt cool under our feet.

_____ **12.** Is that tree a cottonwood?

_____ **13.** The snow will fall quickly tomorrow night.

_____ **14.** He works from early morning to late in the evening.

_____ **15.** Ross and Martha sent a postcard from China.

Direct Objects and Indirect Objects

Direct Objects

4b. A *direct object* is a noun, pronoun, or word group that tells *who* or *what* receives the action of the verb.

>   V   DO
> **EXAMPLES** Do you play **checkers?** [The noun *checkers* receives the action of the verb
>
> *play* and answers the question *Do you play what?*]
>
>   V   DO   DO
> Please follow **him** and **her.** [The pronouns *him* and *her* receive the action
>
> of the verb *follow* and answer the question *Please follow whom?*]
>
>   V   DO
> I have not read ***A Journey to the Center of the Earth*** yet. [The word group
>
> *A Journey to the Center of the Earth* receives the action of the verb *have read*
>
> and answers the question *I have not read what?*]

EXERCISE A Underline the direct object in each of the following sentences. Hint: Some sentences may have more than one direct object.

Examples 1. Did Ellen open the car's <u>hood</u>? [The word *hood* receives the action of the verb *Did*

           open and answers the question *Did Ellen open the what? Hood* is the direct object.]

      2. He ate two <u>sandwiches</u> and a <u>salad</u>. [The words *sandwiches* and *salad* answer the

           question *He ate what? Sandwiches* and *salad* make up the compound direct object.]

1. The other basketball coaches followed her example. [Which word answers the question *The other*

   basketball coaches followed what?]

2. Mark was quickly gathering the branches and leaves. [Which words answer the question *Mark*

   was quickly gathering what?]

3. Will you please mail this?

4. Our whole town celebrates Labor Day at the lake.

5. Those rolls have sesame seeds on them.

6. Can you multiply fractions or decimals?

7. The job was easy and offered good pay, flexible hours, and benefits.

8. A small drop of paint splattered the wall.

9. Generously, she shared her lunch with me.

10. Aunt Jane was wearing her new coat and hat.

GO ON ➡

Indirect Objects

4c. An *indirect object* is a noun, pronoun, or word group that sometimes appears in sentences containing direct objects.

An indirect object answers the question *to* (or *for*) *whom* (or *what*)? after the verb.

>   S   V   IO   DO
> **EXAMPLES** That pep rally showed **everyone** our school spirit! [The pronoun *everyone*
>
> answers the question *The pep rally showed our school spirit to whom?*]
>   S   V   IO
> The pep rally showed the **Midland Middle School Ramblers** the school's
>   **DO**
> appreciation. [The word group *Midland Middle School Ramblers* answers
>
> the question *The pep rally showed the school's appreciation to whom?*]
>   S   V   IO   IO   DO
> Ken sang **Lorna** and **me** that song about the old days. [Both *Lorna* and *me*
>
> answer the question *Ken sang that song about the old days to whom?*]

EXERCISE B Underline the indirect object or indirect objects in each of the following sentences.

Examples 1. Will the PTA buy the camera <u>club</u> a scanner? [Will the PTA buy a scanner for whom? For *club*. *Club* is the indirect object.]

      2. We bought our <u>dog</u> a new collar. [We bought a new collar for what? For *dog*. *Dog* is the indirect object.]

11. Please bring Dad a glass of ice water. [Bring a glass of ice water to whom?]

12. Our friend sent my brother and me a few seashells from Jamaica. [Our friend sent a few seashells from Jamaica to whom?]

13. The coach presented Martin the Most Valuable Player award.

14. A local club offered Pierce Middle School transportation to the national finals.

15. Will you show the world a better way?

16. The crowd gave the singer a loud cheer.

17. Your help saved us plenty of time.

18. She bought Juanita and Mike new calculators.

19. We can teach them a lesson about soccer.

20. The landlord promised Mrs. Baker and him new faucets.

Predicate Nominatives

4e. A *predicate nominative* is a word or word group in the predicate that identifies the subject.

A predicate nominative appears only in a sentence that has a linking verb. Common linking verbs include *is, was, will be, could have been,* and *has been.*

EXAMPLES   The first performers on stage will be the **band.** [The noun *band* identifies the subject *performers.*]

Could the singer have been **she**? [The pronoun *she* identifies the subject *singer.*]

My favorite book has always been ***The Old Man and the Sea.*** [The word group *The Old Man and the Sea* identifies the subject *book.*]

EXERCISE A   Underline the predicate nominative in each of the following sentences.

Example 1. The first subway system in the world was the London Underground. [*London Underground* identifies the subject, *system. London Underground* is the predicate nominative.]

1. The skyscraper will be our landmark. [What word identifies the subject *skyscraper*?]

2. You could become friends with each other.

3. Mitchell will be the first one in line as usual.

4. She will be treasurer for only two more weeks.

5. The most popular place for seafood was Neptune Sammy's Restaurant.

TIP To find the predicate nominative in a question, turn the question into a statement.

| | V | S | | V | PN | |
QUESTION   Has George always been our expert on math?

| | S | V | | V | PN | |
STATEMENT   George has always been our expert on math. [The word order of the statement makes it easier to tell that *expert* is the predicate nominative.]

EXERCISE B   Underline the predicate nominative in each of the following sentences.

Examples 1. Isn't *Ben Hur* your favorite movie? [*Movie* identifies the subject *Ben Hur. Movie* is the predicate nominative.]

2. Luisa is vice-president of the student council. [*Vice-president* identifies the subject *Luisa. Vice-president* is the predicate nominative.]

6. This is the best book in the series. [Which word identifies the subject *This*?]

7. Will Teresa be the club's next president? [Which word identifies the subject *Teresa*?]

Developmental Language Skills

8. Anyone can become anything.

9. With hard work, he will soon be a fluent speaker of Japanese.

10. The winner of the 1993 Nobel Prize in literature was Toni Morrison from the United States.

11. That was really something!

12. He was a young king but ruled wisely.

13. They remained citizens for many years.

14. Have you always been a fan of theirs?

15. Mr. Perez has been a teacher for many years.

A linking verb may have more than one predicate nominative. Two or more predicate nominatives of the same linking verb are called a *compound predicate nominative.*

> **EXAMPLE**   George has always been our **expert** and **advisor** on math. [Both *expert* and *advisor* identify the subject *George*. Together, *expert* and *advisor* make up the compound predicate nominative.]

EXERCISE C Underline the compound predicate nominatives in each of the following sentences.

Example 1. Is the capital of Australia <u>Sydney</u> or <u>Canberra</u>? [*Sydney* and *Canberra* both identify the

subject, *capital. Sydney* and *Canberra* are both predicate nominatives.]

16. My stepmother is a good manager and a great friend. [Which two words identify the subject

stepmother?]

17. The best trainers with the bird dogs are Manny and she. [Which two words identify the subject

trainers?]

18. Will you become an inventor, a writer, or a mechanic?

19. Was the most important ingredient cornmeal or flour?

20. The next course should be Art History 2 or Drawing 2.

21. Darla is my sister and tutor.

22. Two Australian cities are Sydney and Perth.

23. For three years, Mrs. Chen has been my coach and friend.

24. Were the winners of the contest Matt and Lucinda?

25. The flying animals are insects, bats, and birds.

Predicate Adjectives

4f. A **predicate adjective** is an adjective that is in the predicate and that describes the subject.

Like a predicate nominative, a predicate adjective completes the meaning of a linking verb. Predicate adjectives follow linking verbs such as *is, are, seem, appear, feel, sound,* and *smell.*

> **EXAMPLES** The Rodriguezes are **happy** about their new home. [The adjective *happy* describes the subject *Rodriguezes* and completes the meaning of the linking verb *are.* Therefore, *happy* is a predicate adjective.]
>
> Doesn't the soup smell **delicious?** [The adjective *delicious* describes the subject *soup* and completes the meaning of the linking verb *smell.* Therefore, *delicious* is a predicate adjective.]

REMINDER▶ An adjective is word that describes a person, place, thing, or idea. An adjective usually answers the question *what kind?, how many?, how much?,* or *which one?*

EXERCISE A Underline the predicate adjective in each of the following sentences.

Example 1. That Japanese tea set looks <u>expensive</u>. [The adjective *expensive* describes the subject *tea set. Expensive* is the predicate adjective.]

1. Her purple cape felt smooth. [Which word describes the subject *cape*?]

2. That lemonade tastes sour.

3. Those exercises were easy.

4. Along the horizon the sky looked orange.

5. Did that bird look frightening to you?

A linking verb may have more than one predicate adjective. Two or more predicate adjectives that complete the meaning of the same linking verb are called a **compound predicate adjective.**

> **EXAMPLE** How **happy** and **excited** Cynthia sounded about their move to Phoenix! [The adjectives *happy* and *excited* both describe the subject *Cynthia* and complete the meaning of the linking verb *sounded.*]

EXERCISE B Underline the predicate adjective or predicate adjectives in each of the following sentences.

Example 1. The cantaloupe tasted <u>sweet</u> and <u>ripe</u> to me. [The adjectives *sweet* and *ripe* describe the subject *cantaloupe* and complete the meaning of the linking verb *tasted.*]

6. Pine needles smell sharp and fresh. [Which two words describe the subject *needles*?]

7. Something in that engine sounds wrong.

8. That Labrador retriever is quite smart and lovable.

9. Are you free this afternoon?

10. The kindergartners seemed eager but shy.

NOTE Do not mistake an adverb for a predicate adjective. As you may remember, most adverbs describe a verb. Predicate adjectives do not describe verbs. Almost all predicate adjectives describe a person, place, or thing.

ADVERB	They worked **hard.** [*Hard* describes the verb *worked. Hard* tells *how* they worked.]
PREDICATE ADJECTIVE	Their work was **hard.** [*Hard* describes the subject *work. Hard* tells *what kind* of work.]

EXERCISE C Underline the predicate adjective or predicate adjectives in each of the following sentences.

Example 1. On some remote islands, birds are <u>wild</u> but completely <u>unafraid</u> of humans.

[The adjectives *wild* and *unafraid* describe the subject *birds. Wild* and *unafraid* are the

predicate adjectives.]

11. Somehow the antique table had remained clean and undamaged. [Which words in the predicate

describe the subject *table*?]

12. Is Paul older or younger than his sister? [Which words in the predicate describe the subject *Paul*?]

13. How beautiful the flute music in the distance sounded!

14. Your clay should be moist and soft.

15. In my opinion, the car on that magazine cover is incredible.

16. The tortilla soup at my favorite restaurant tastes spicy.

17. Just after the snow, Summit Lane seemed bright and clean.

18. The flowers were both beautiful and fragrant.

19. Will the test tomorrow be easy or hard?

20. To the people on shore, the waves looked calm.

The Phrase

5a. A *phrase* is a group of related words that is used as a single part of speech. A phrase does not contain both a subject and a verb.

VERB PHRASE	may be asking [This phrase has no subject.]
PREPOSITIONAL PHRASE	through the forest [This phrase has no subject or verb.]
INFINITIVE PHRASE	to travel to India [This phrase has no subject or verb. *To travel* is an infinitive, not a main verb.]

REMINDER Phrases act the same way that single words do within sentences.

EXAMPLES   My sister **may be asking** for your help. [The phrase *may be asking* acts as the verb and tells something about *sister*.]

We walked **through the forest.** [The phrase *through the forest* acts as an adverb and modifies the verb *walked*.]

Samuel wants **to travel to India.** [The phrase *to travel to India* acts as the direct object and tells what Samuel wants.]

Remembering my last vacation, I wrote an essay for my English class. [The phrase *Remembering my last vacation* acts as an adjective and describes the subject *I*.]

NOTE If a word group has both a subject and a verb, it is not a phrase.

EXAMPLES   the **children played** [*Children* is the subject of the verb *played*.]

after the **boy arrived** [*Boy* is the subject of the verb *arrived*.]

EXERCISE A Identify each of the following word groups as a phrase or not a phrase. On the lines provided, write *P* for *phrase* or *NP* for *not a phrase*.

Examples ___P___ **1.** near the statue [This word group does not contain subject or a verb. The word group is a phrase.]

___NP___ **2.** before we go there [This word group contains a verb, *go*, and its subject, *we*. The word group is not a phrase.]

_____ **1.** on the hot roof [Does this word group contain a subject and a verb?]

_____ **2.** after they called [Does this word group contain a subject and a verb?]

_____ **3.** under a clear, blue sky

_____ **4.** was talking

_____ **5.** had been heard

_____ **6.** since we know her

_____ **7.** under the table

_____ **8.** as you can see

_____ **9.** to store at room temperature

_____ **10.** watching the game

_____ **11.** with much effort

_____ **12.** how I did it

GO ON

_____ **13.** when the song started   _____ **17.** above the refrigerator

_____ **14.** to try a different way   _____ **18.** to explore a new route

_____ **15.** to another place   _____ **19.** before school ends

_____ **16.** around the corner   _____ **20.** where they stood

EXERCISE B Identify each of the following underlined word groups as a phrase or not a phrase. Write *P* for *phrase* or *NP* for *not a phrase* on the line provided.

Examples __P__ **1.** Claire rode her bicycle down the hill. [The underlined word group does not

have a subject or a verb. This word group is a phrase.]

__NP__ **2.** That book belongs to Mary. [The underlined word group does have a subject

and a verb. This word group is not a phrase.]

_____ **21.** To teach young children is my sister's goal. [Does the underlined word group have both a

subject and a verb?]

_____ **22.** Next summer my family will be going to the beach. [Does the underlined word group

have both a subject and a verb?]

_____ **23.** Jogging slowly, Max controlled his breathing.

_____ **24.** Trevor, clearly delighted by the good news, jumped with joy.

_____ **25.** The pictures taken yesterday will be developed by noon today.

_____ **26.** Before the concert, we should all meet at the fountain.

_____ **27.** Stacey and Melinda want to join a bird-watching club.

_____ **28.** With great effort, the mountain climber reached the top.

_____ **29.** The lake near our town has many varieties of fish.

_____ **30.** The best person to help you is probably Lori.

The Prepositional Phrase

Prepositional Phrases

5b. A ***prepositional phrase*** includes a preposition, the object of the preposition, and any modifiers of that object.

A *preposition* is a word that shows the relationship of a noun or a pronoun to another word. The *object of the preposition* is the noun or pronoun that completes the prepositional phrase.

> | | P | OP |
> EXAMPLES   with someone [The preposition is *with*. The object of the preposition is
>
> *someone. Someone* is not modified by any words.]
>
> | P | | OP |
> to the popular author's address [The preposition is *to*. The object of the
>
> preposition is *address. Address* is modified by *the popular author's*.]
>
> | P | OP | OP |
> along with him and his son [The preposition is *along with*. The objects of
>
> the preposition are *him* and *son. Son* is modified by *his*.]

EXERCISE A Underline the prepositional phrase in each of the following sentences.

Example 1. Matzo is a bread that is made <u>without yeast</u>. [The preposition is *without*. The object of the preposition is *yeast*.]

1. Landscapes and mountain scenes like these are especially beautiful. [Which word is a preposition? Which word is the object of that preposition?]

2. One of the boys spoke French.

3. Wow! They play well for beginners.

4. White, wispy clouds danced in the sky.

5. Under the bed was my old journal.

Adjective Phrases

An ***adjective phrase*** is a prepositional phrase that modifies a noun or a pronoun. An adjective phrase answers the same questions that an adjective answers: *What kind? Which one? How many?* or *How much?*

> EXAMPLES   Take the seat **by Mr. Davis.** [The adjective phrase *by Mr. Davis* modifies
>
> the noun *seat* by telling *which seat*.]
>
> Some **of the books** were overdue. [The adjective phrase *of the books*
>
> modifies the pronoun *Some* by telling *which ones*.]

GO ON

EXERCISE B For each of the following sentences, underline the adjective phrase. Then, draw two lines under the word that the phrase modifies.

Example 1. Three of the trees are sprouting new branches. [The preposition is *of* and the object of the preposition is *trees*. The prepositional phrase modifies *Three*.]

6. Check the cabinet under the sink. [Which word is a preposition? Which word is the object of that preposition? Which word does the prepositional phrase modify?]

7. The other students in my class are very friendly.

8. A squirrel on the top branch chattered noisily.

9. David just finished a book about redwood forests.

10. Have you wrapped that present for your mother?

Adverb Phrases

An *adverb phrase* is a prepositional phrase that modifies a verb, an adjective, or an adverb. An adverb phrase answers the same questions that an adverb answers: *Where? When? How? Why? How often? How long? To what extent? Under what conditions?* or *How much?*

EXAMPLES Sit **by Mr. Davis.** [The adverb phrase *by Mr. Davis* modifies the verb *Sit* by telling *where?*]

Math is easy **for him and me.** [The adverb phrase *for him and me* modifies the adjective *easy* by telling *how?*]

Late **in the afternoon,** the mail arrived. [The adverb phrase *in the afternoon* modifies the adverb *Late* by telling *when?*]

EXERCISE C For each of the following sentences, underline the adverb phrase. Then, draw two lines under the word or words that the phrase modifies.

Example 1. Down the car's side, a white pinstripe had been painted. [The preposition is *down* and the object of the preposition is *side*. The prepositional phrase modifies the verb phrase *had been painted* by telling *where?*]

11. Deep blue metallic paint glistened in the sunlight. [Which word is a preposition? Which word is the object of that preposition? Which word does the prepositional phrase modify?]

12. Under the hood, everything had been cleaned.

13. Several people helped on weekends.

14. These changes had been made by the sixth owner and some friends.

15. In time, the car will look brand new.

The Participle and the Participial Phrase
Participles

5e.   A *participle* is a verb form that can be used as an adjective.

> **EXAMPLES**   a **shining** smile [The participle *shining* describes the noun *smile.*]
>
> his **wrinkled** brow [The participle *wrinkled* describes the noun *brow.*]
>
> the **broken** one [The participle *broken* describes the pronoun *one.*]

> **NOTE** There are two types of participles—present participles and past participles. All present participles end in *–ing.* However, the form of past participles is not always the same. Notice in the examples above that past participles may end in *–ed* or *–en* or *–t.* Some past participles are formed in other ways.

A participle may come before or after the word that it modifies.

> **EXAMPLES**   The crowd remained **standing.**
>
> **Standing,** the crowd applauded.
>
> The **standing** crowd applauded wildly.

EXERCISE A Underline the participle in each of the following sentences.

Examples 1. Beneath the porch, the cat hid from the <u>pouring</u> rain. [*Pouring* is a participle that describes the noun *rain.*]

2. <u>Honored</u>, she accepted the award. [*Honored* is a participle that describes the pronoun *she.*]

1. Oh, no. I smell burnt toast again. [Which word is a verb form that describes a noun?]

2. Add two beaten eggs to the mixture. [Which word is a verb form that describes a noun?]

3. They need two signed copies of the contract.

4. Have you found the lost remote control yet?

5. What is a "running foot" anyway?

6. One excited little girl could hardly stand still.

7. Exhausted, she stumbled across the finish line.

8. A folding chair sat beside the door.

9. Ten dripping shirts hung from the line.

10. Carved stones lined the garden bed.

GO ON

Participial Phrases

| **5f.** | A *participial phrase* consists of a participle together with its modifiers and complements. The entire phrase is used as an adjective. |

A participle can be modified by an adverb and by a prepositional phrase. A participial phrase can also have a complement and all of the complement's modifiers. A complement is a word that completes the meaning of a verb. *Direct objects* and *indirect objects* complete the meaning of an action verb. *Predicate nominatives* and *predicate adjectives* complete the meaning of linking verbs.

> **EXAMPLES** Mr. Johnson, **being a tall man,** was not comfortable in the small car. [The participle *being* is completed by the predicate nominative *man*. *Man* is modified by the adjectives *a* and *tall*. The entire participial phrase is used as an adjective to modify the noun *Mr. Johnson*.]
>
> **Giving us a copy of the report,** Jim began his speech. [The participle *Giving* has an indirect object, *us*, and a direct object, *copy*. The direct object is modified by an article, *a*, and a prepositional phrase, *of the report*. The entire participial phrase is used as an adjective to modify the noun *Jim*.]

EXERCISE B Underline the participial phrase in each of the following sentences.

Examples 1. <u>Done with his tricks and stunts,</u> the clown accepted everyone's applause. [*Done* is a participle that describes *clown*. *With his tricks and stunts* is a prepositional phrase modifying *Done*.]

2. Charcoal grills <u>glowing with embers</u> dotted the park. [*Glowing* is a participle that describes *grills*. *With embers* is a prepositional phrase that modifies *glowing*.]

11. Streaming into the starry sky, fireworks exploded over the bay. [Which word is a verb form that describes *fireworks*? Which prepositional phrase modifies that word?]

12. "Seventy-six Trombones" blared from a band performing onstage. [Which word is a verb form that describes *band*? Which word modifies that word?]

13. Blankets laid out over the grass held small family groups.

14. Picnic tables were covered with food and ice chests holding cold drinks.

15. Some dogs chased a ball decorated with red and white stripes.

16. Later, a group of American Indians dancing in full costume entertained the crowd.

17. Earlier, a dozen Thai girls had performed an elegant dance handed down for generations.

18. Unpacking their instruments, a Dixieland jazz band got ready for their turn.

19. A group of folk dancers, specially flown in from San Antonio, swirled in a rainbow of skirts.

20. Sleepily nodding in car seats, children and babies were driven home.

The Infinitive and the Infinitive Phrase

Infinitives

5g. An *infinitive* is a verb form that can be used as a noun, an adjective, or an adverb. Most infinitives begin with *to*.

NOUN	**To paint** is his only ambition. [The infinitive *To paint* is the subject of the verb *is*.]
	The puppy only wants **to play.** [The infinitive *to play* is the direct object of the verb *wants*.]
	His dream was **to fly.** [The infinitive *to fly* is the predicate nominative of the verb *was*.]
ADJECTIVE	She's the swimmer **to watch.** [The infinitive *to watch* modifies the noun *swimmer*.]
	The one **to ask** is he. [The infinitive *to ask* modifies the pronoun *one*.]
ADVERB	**To exit,** simply press the escape key. [The infinitive *To exit* modifies the verb *press*.]
	It is easy **to find.** [The infinitive *to find* modifies the adjective *easy*.]

NOTE▶ *To* can also be used as a preposition.

EXAMPLE	She went **to** the store **to** shop. [The first *to* is followed by a noun, *store*, so it is being used as a preposition. The second *to* is followed by a verb form, *shop*, so it is being used as part of an infinitive.]

EXERCISE A Underline the infinitive in each of the following sentences.

Examples 1. The right to vote is very valuable. [*To* is followed by the verb *vote*. *To vote* is the infinitive.]

2. To succeed, you must work very hard. [*To* is followed by the verb *succeed*. *To succeed* is the infinitive.]

1. I tried to call but the line was busy. [Is *to* followed by a verb?]

2. Their only goal is to excel. [Is *to* followed by a verb?]

3. Is this dresser very heavy to lift?

4. Here is the number to call.

5. To finish will be a relief.

6. Did you agree with the decision to go?

7. This case will not be easy to solve.

8. To fly, the wings must create more lift.

GO ON ➡

9. Michael is learning to type.

10. Jason already went to the cafeteria to eat.

Infinitive Phrases

5h. An *infinitive phrase* consists of an infinitive together with its modifiers and complements. The entire phrase may be used as a noun, an adjective, or an adverb.

NOUN	She always wants **to be sure.** [The infinitive *to be* is completed by the predicate adjective *sure.* The infinitive phrase is used as the direct object of the verb *wants.*]
ADJECTIVE	This would be a perfect time **to start a club.** [The infinitive *to start* is completed by the direct object *club.* The infinitive phrase modifies the noun *time.*]
ADVERB	We gathered in the park **to clean up after the Founders' Day picnic.** [The infinitive *to clean* is modified by the adverb *up* and by the adverb phrase *after the Founders' Day picnic.* The infinitive phrase modifies the verb *gathered.*]

EXERCISE B Underline the infinitive phrase in each of the following sentences.

Examples 1. To type well requires steady practice. [*To* is followed by the verb *type.* *Type* is modified by the adverb *well.* The infinitive phrase is *To type well.*]

2. We need a ramp to get wheelchairs into the auditorium. [*To* is followed by the verb *get.* *Get* is completed by the direct object *wheelchairs* and is modified by the adverb phrase *into the auditorium.* The infinitive phrase is *to get wheelchairs into the auditorium.*]

11. To eat nutritious meals and snacks is important to good health. [Is *To* followed by a verb? What words modify or complete that verb?]

12. You're too smart to fall for that old joke! [Is *to* followed by a verb? What words modify that verb?]

13. They had planned to practice all weekend.

14. Right now, your major goal is to do well in school.

15. Actually, the equation is simple to solve without a calculator.

16. Try to use more colors and shapes.

17. We need some community service projects to put in our portfolios.

18. The solution was to exit the program and reboot.

19. I'm so sorry to be late for our appointment.

20. Do you really need to play basketball at six o'clock in the morning, Toby?

Appositives and Appositive Phrases
Appositives

5i. | An **appositive** is a noun or pronoun used to explain or identify another noun or pronoun.

> **EXAMPLES** We **teenagers** do enjoy sports. [*Teenagers* identifies the pronoun *We.*]
>
> You can get that information from only one person, **her.** [*Her* identifies the noun *person.*]

An appositive usually follows the noun or pronoun it identifies. However, sometimes an appositive comes before the noun or pronoun it modifiers.

> **EXAMPLE** **A painter,** Tom paid careful attention to details.

NOTE Two or more appositives may refer back to the same word.

> **EXAMPLE** The twins, **Mary and Michelle,** will play in the doubles match. [Both *Mary* and *Michelle* are appositives for the noun *twins.*]

EXERCISE A Underline the appositive in each of the following sentences.

Examples 1. Her dog, <u>Dusty</u>, must have known fifty tricks. [The appositive *Dusty* identifies the noun *dog.*]

2. Can you recognize the constellation <u>Little Dipper</u>? [The appositive *Little Dipper* identifies the noun *constellation.*]

1. Their favorite magazine, *National Geographic*, sat in stacks along the wall. [Which words identify the noun *magazine*?]

2. Can you play the game chess? [Which word identifies another noun?]

3. Have you asked your cousin Judy about the movie?

4. Only one person, you, can make that decision.

5. My brother Sam collects bottle caps.

6. Tom's favorite song, "Over the Rainbow," was playing on the radio.

7. I could talk for hours with my friend Trevor.

8. The rose Caroline's Fancy was named for my grandmother.

9. He came in on the freighter *Anabelle Lee*.

10. Were they with their brothers Stan and Carl?

Appositive Phrases

5j. An *appositive phrase* includes an appositive together with all of its modifiers.

An appositive may be modified by adjectives, phrases, and even clauses. The appositive phrase includes the appositive and all its modifiers.

> **EXAMPLES** Frank, **the starting quarterback in tonight's game,** may break a school record this season. [The appositive is *quarterback. Quarterback* is modified by *the, starting,* and *in tonight's game.* Together, these words make up the appositive phrase.]
>
> My great-grandfather is Mr. Doe, **a wise man who is one hundred years old.** [The appositive is *man. Man* is modified by *a, wise,* and *who is one hundred years old.* Together, these words make up the appositive phrase.]

EXERCISE B Underline the appositive phrase in each of the following sentences.

Examples 1. This computer chip, <u>the first of its kind</u>, promises much faster calculations. [The appositive phrase *the first of its kind* explains the noun *chip.*]

2. <u>A classic model from the 1950s</u>, the black convertible drew a crowd. [The appositive phrase *A classic model from the 1950s* explains the noun *convertible.*]

11. Janet, the only student from our district who made it to the state finals, has been studying hard. [Which phrase explains a noun in the sentence?]

12. The fawn, one of a pair, struggled to its feet. [Which phrase explains a noun in the sentence?]

13. Have you met our new neighbor Mrs. Wendell?

14. I just received a letter from Mario, my penpal from Italy.

15. Take these to Mr. Lincoln, our new secretary.

16. Mark Twain, author of *The Adventures of Tom Sawyer,* also wrote many short stories.

17. The audience really enjoyed the guest speaker, an expert on astronomy.

18. Dan watched *A Bug's Life,* his favorite movie, again last weekend.

19. The geography of three countries, Germany, France, and Spain, was Rick's topic.

20. The trophy, a symbol of the team's hard work, was displayed near the school's front door.

Independent and Subordinate Clauses

The Independent Clause

6a. | A **clause** is a word group that contains a verb and its subject and that is used as a sentence or as part of a sentence.

When you think of a clause, remember this combination: subject and verb. When you see a word group that has a subject and its verb, you're looking at a clause. In other words, every clause has a subject and verb.

>   **S**   **V**
> **CLAUSES**   Whose **jacket is** in the hallway? [This word group has a subject, *jacket*, and
>
> a verb, *is*. For this reason, the word group is a clause.]
>   **S**   **V**
> because **we will try** our best [This word group has a subject, *we*, and a
>
> verb, *will try*. For this reason, the word group is a clause.]

EXERCISE A Underline the verb in each clause below. Then, circle the subject of that verb.

Example 1. (who) is the best actress [The clause contains the verb *is*. *Who* is the subject of *is*.]

1. we play soccer every Saturday [Which word shows an action? Which word shows who is doing the action?]

2. while Jon waits

3. after we return from Kansas

4. Kelly mowed the lawn yesterday

5. those lyrics were written by Francis Scott Key

Every clause has a subject and a verb. However, not every clause expresses a complete thought. There are two kinds of clauses—clauses that *do* express a complete thought and clauses that do *not* express a complete thought.

6b. | An **independent** (or **main**) **clause** expresses a complete thought and can stand by itself as a sentence.

>   **S**   **V**
> **INDEPENDENT CLAUSES**   **Rocky Mountain National Park is** in Colorado. [The subject is *Rocky*
>
> *Mountain National Park*, and the verb is *is*. Does the word group express
>
> a complete thought? Yes, so the word group is an independent clause.]
>   **V** **S** **V**
> **Will we run** laps in gym class tomorrow morning? [The subject is *we*, and
>
> the verb is *Will run*. Does the word group express a complete thought?
>
> Yes, so the word group is an independent clause.]

GO ON

EXERCISE B Write *I* on the line before each word group below that is an independent clause. Leave the line blank for each word group that is not an independent clause. Then, make each independent clause a sentence by capitalizing the first letter and adding an end mark.

Example _____*I*_____ **1.** is Frankfort the capital of Kentucky? [This word group has a subject, *Frankfort*,

and a verb, *is*, and it does express a complete thought.]

_____ **6.** koalas have sharp claws [Does this word group express a complete thought?]

_____ **7.** on a trail through the meadow

_____ **8.** an ant near our picnic basket

_____ **9.** with great energy and strength

_____**10.** have you ever been to a dog show

The Subordinate Clause

6c. A *subordinate* (or *dependent*) *clause* has a subject and its verb but does not express a complete thought and cannot stand by itself as a complete sentence.

A subordinate clause is incomplete until it is connected to at least one independent clause. Subordinate clauses almost always begin with a connecting word, such as *because, when, that, who,* or *if.* This connecting word helps connect a subordinate clause to an independent clause.

SUBORDINATE CLAUSE when the **elk grew** antlers [The subject is *elk*, the verb is *grew*, and the

connecting word is *when*. The word group does not express a complete

thought, so the word group is a subordinate clause.]

EXERCISE C Each sentence below has an independent clause and a subordinate clause. Underline the subordinate clause, and circle the connecting word.

Example 1. (Because) they like vegetables, Mom and Dad had a salad for lunch. [*Because they like*

vegetables starts with the connecting word *Because* and does not express a complete

thought. That word group is the subordinate clause.]

11. When the rainstorm started, the children put on their coats. [What part of the sentence begins

with a connecting word and does not make sense by itself?]

12. The sun was in my eyes until I put on this baseball cap.

13. Before CDs were invented, cassette tapes were popular.

14. Let's watch the video that you rented.

15. When you finish painting your canvas, put your art supplies back in the cabinet, everyone!

The Adjective Clause

6c. A *subordinate* (or *dependent*) *clause* does not express a complete thought and cannot stand by itself as a complete sentence.

SUBORDINATE CLAUSE   which had climbed the tree [The subordinate clause has a subject, *which*, and a verb, *had climbed*, but it cannot stand alone as a complete sentence.]

One type of subordinate clause is the *adjective clause*. Like adjectives, adjective clauses can describe a person, place, thing, or idea. An adjective clause usually follows the word or words it describes. The clause tells *which one* or *what kind*.

EXAMPLES   The new student **whom we met yesterday** will be in our homeroom. [The adjective clause *whom we met yesterday* tells *which* student.]

Ricardo bought a book **that tells the life story of painter Diego Rivera.**

[The adjective clause *that tells the life story of painter Diego Rivera* tells *what kind* of book.]

EXERCISE A Draw an arrow from the underlined adjective clause to the word that the adjective clause describes.

Example 1. Can the project, which requires a drill, be completed in a day? [*Which requires a drill* describes *project* by telling *what kind*.]

1. Here is the friend whom I mentioned. [Which word is described by the clause *whom I mentioned*?]

2. Banyan trees, which originally grew in India, thrive in Florida.

3. How was the movie that you and Al saw?

4. Applause should go to the engineers, who worked hard on the airplane's design.

5. Did the book that you just read change your view on life?

Adjective clauses usually begin with connecting words. These connecting words are called *relative pronouns.* A relative pronoun helps connect an adjective clause to an independent clause. Common relative pronouns are *that, which, who, whom,* and *whose.*

                                                                        RP
EXAMPLES   An ostrich, **which is the fastest bird on land,** can run up to forty miles per hour. [The relative pronoun *which* connects the adjective clause to the independent clause. The adjective clause *which is the fastest bird on land* describes the noun *ostrich.*]

Developmental Language Skills

RP

Does the hat **that is on the table** belong to you? [The relative

pronoun *that* connects the adjective clause to the independent clause.

The adjective clause *that is on the table* describes the noun *hat*.]

EXERCISE B Circle the relative pronoun in each sentence below. Each adjective clause has been underlined for you.

Example 1. Put these cans in the bag (that) the food bank gave us. [The relative pronoun *that*

connects the adjective clause to the independent clause.]

6. She is the teacher who is in charge of the music program. [Which word connects the adjective

clause to the independent clause?]

7. The woman whom the computer store recommended is on the phone.

8. The job went to Terry, whose education included computer classes.

9. Bobcats, which live in North America, are wildcats with long legs.

10. Is this the tie that he liked?

EXERCISE C Underline the adjective clause in each of the following sentences.

Example 1. The trip that we planned was for five days. [The relative pronoun is *that*. The verb is

planned, and its subject is *we*. There are no other words in the adjective clause.]

11. Kyle, whose mother has a van, was in charge of provisions. [Look for the relative pronoun.

Then, find the subject and verb that follow it.]

12. Our trip was planned by Martin, who is good with maps.

13. The trip, which was Eddie's first, would begin at 5:00 A.M.

14. We walked carefully on the trail that led up the mountain.

15. Where are the photographs that show our mountain campsite?

The Adverb Clause

6c. A *subordinate* (or *dependent*) *clause* does not express a complete thought and cannot stand by itself as a complete sentence.

SUBORDINATE CLAUSE   because his tooth hurt [This clause has a subject, *tooth*, and a verb, *hurt*, but it does not express a complete thought, so it is a subordinate clause.]

One type of subordinate clause is the **adverb clause.** Like adverbs, adverb clauses describe a verb, an adjective, or an adverb. Adverb clauses answer the following questions: *How? When? Where? Why? To what extent? How much? How long?* and *Under what conditions?*

Adverb clauses begin with words such as the following:

after	as soon as	in order that	until
although	as though	since	when
as	because	so that	whenever
as if	before	than	where
as long as	how	though	wherever
as much as	if	unless	while

These words connect an adverb clause to the rest of the sentence.

EXAMPLES   Katy knocked on the door **until someone opened it.** [The adverb clause describes the verb *knocked*. This clause tells *how long* Katy knocked. The word *until* begins the adverb clause and connects it to the rest of the sentence.]

I laughed more loudly **than I had intended.** [The adverb clause describes the adverb *more*. This clause tells *to what extent* I laughed more loudly. The word *than* begins the adverb clause and connects it to the rest of the sentence.]

EXERCISE A The adverb clause in each of the following sentences has been underlined for you. Circle the word that connects the adverb clause to the rest of the sentence. Hint: The connecting word usually comes at the beginning of an adverb clause.

Example 1. Does Fiona's golden retriever bark loudly (whenever) it is outside? [The connecting word *whenever* comes at the beginning of the adverb clause.]

1. If the roads are icy, we will stay home. [What word comes at the beginning of the adverb clause?]

2. We won't arrive on time unless we leave home immediately.

3. The clothing at that thrift store was more stylish than I had expected.

4. Until you have seen a bald eagle, you may not appreciate its beauty.

5. Did Jen play guitar while Ed sang?

To find an adverb clause, look for the following things in a sentence. If you can answer *yes* to all the questions below, you have probably found an adverb clause.

- Can you find a connecting word (such as *after, because,* or *than*)?
- Do a subject and its verb follow the connecting word?
- Does the group of words contain a connecting word, a subject, and its verb?
- Does the word group describe a verb, and adjective, or an adverb?

NOTE Adverb clauses may be placed in various positions in sentences. When an adverb clause comes at the beginning of a sentence, it is usually followed by a comma.

EXERCISE B Underline the adverb clause in each of the following sentences. Hint: Remember that adverb clauses usually begin with a connecting word.

Examples 1. After Tim saved fifty dollars, he put it in the bank. [The adverb clause begins with the connecting word *After* and has a subject, *Tim,* and a verb, *saved.*]

2. The VCR will not work if we hook up the cords incorrectly. [The adverb clause begins with the connecting word *if* and has a subject, *we,* and a verb, *hook.*]

6. The crowd stood for the national anthem before the football game began. [Which word can be a connecting word? Is it followed by a verb and its subject?]

7. As long as they are quiet, the children can watch the movie with us. [Which words can be connecting words? Are they followed by a verb and its subject?]

8. There were muddy footprints wherever Natalie had walked.

9. The delicate hummingbird flapped its wings as it flew near the flowers.

10. Because Maria likes comic books, she has a large comic-book collection.

11. Pumpkin seeds are tastier if you toast them.

12. When the river flowed through this area, the water created this valley.

13. Because Willis has studied the fifty states, he knows special facts about each one.

14. If Megan runs in the race this weekend, will she finish in first place?

15. The ground was gray and slushy where a field of snow had not melted yet.

Sentence Structure: Simple Sentences; Compound Sentences

Simple Sentences

7a. A **simple sentence** contains one independent clause and no subordinate clauses.

An independent clause has a subject and a verb. It expresses a complete thought. An independent clause can stand alone as a sentence.

                                                            S   V

EXAMPLES The entire **family had gathered** for dinner. [This entire sentence is an

independent clause. *Family* is the subject, and *had gathered* is the verb.]

                        V

Please **send** me e-mail this weekend. [In this sentence, the subject is

understood to be *you*, and the verb is *send*.]

EXERCISE A Draw one line under the subject and two lines under the verb in each of the following sentences.

Example _____ **1.** <u>Cedric</u> <u><u>put</u></u> on his bike helmet. [The subject is *Cedric* and the verb is *put*.]

_____ **1.** The old, tall tree fell. [Which word is the subject? Which word is the verb?]

_____ **2.** Did Mary see the elephants at the zoo?

_____ **3.** Before lunch, Bianca went to the lake.

_____ **4.** The dragon in that movie looked so realistic!

_____ **5.** Everybody agreed on the best solution to the problem.

A simple sentence may have a compound subject, a compound verb, or both.

                                S   S   V   V

EXAMPLE The brave **men** and **women rescued** everyone and **saved** the building.

[*Men* and *women* make up the compound subject and *rescued* and *saved*

make up the compound verb in this sentence.]

EXERCISE B Draw one line under the subject and two lines under the verb in each of the following sentences. Hint: Some sentences have a compound subject, a compound verb, or both.

Example 1. <u>Fran</u> and <u>Roberto</u> <u><u>will climb</u></u> the mountain and <u><u>will rest</u></u> at its peak. [*Fran* and *Roberto*

make up the compound subject, and *will climb* and *will rest* make up the compound verb.]

6. Don and Mary wear special glasses for sports. [Draw one line under both of the people the

sentence is about. Draw two lines under the word that tells what happens.]

7. My aunt and uncle live in Southern California.

8. The sun shines through my window every morning.

9. Where is your grandfather's house?

10. Mom and Dad roasted a chicken and baked fresh bread for dinner.

Compound Sentences

7b.   A *compound sentence* contains two or more independent clauses and no subordinate clauses.

The independent clauses of a compound sentence are usually joined together by a comma and a connecting word (*and, but, or, nor, for, so,* or *yet*). The independent clauses of a compound sentence may be connected by a semicolon (;). When a semicolon joins together two independent clauses, no connecting word is needed.

>   S V   S V
> **EXAMPLES** **Egypt is a country in Africa,** and **Argentina is a country in South America.**
>
> [This compound sentence contains two independent clauses. The two clauses are joined by a comma and the connecting word *and*.]
>
>   S V   S   V
> **Koko is a famous lowland gorilla; she communicates in American Sign**
>
> **Language.** [In this compound sentence, a semicolon joins together the two independent clauses.]

EXERCISE C Each sentence below has two independent clauses that are joined together. Draw one line under both independent clauses in each sentence below. Then, circle the item or items that join the two clauses together.

Example 1. Mandy and Anna opened their lockers; they pulled out several books. [The word group *Mandy and Anna opened their lockers* is an independent clause because it has a subject and verb and expresses a complete thought. The word group *they pulled out several books* is an independent clause because it has a subject and a verb and expresses a complete thought. A semicolon joins the two clauses together.]

11. Dennis cleaned the kitchen, and John folded the laundry. [Which two word groups have a subject and a verb and express a complete thought? What punctuation mark and connecting word join the two clauses together?]

12. The skaters wore safety helmets; they also wore kneepads and elbow pads.

13. A flock of geese was flying south, for winter was approaching.

14. Seven runners will compete, but only one can take home the trophy.

15. You can trim the bushes near the house, or you can rake the leaves.

Complex Sentences; Compound-Complex Sentences

Complex Sentences

7c. | A *complex sentence* contains one independent clause and at least one subordinate clause.

An independent clause is a word group that has a subject and a verb and expresses a complete thought. A subordinate clause also has a subject and a verb, but it does not express a complete thought. Subordinate clauses are connected to independent clauses with words such as *who, whom, whose, which, that, after, as, because, if, since,* and *when.*

INDEPENDENT CLAUSE Last night I saw the play. [This word group has a subject and a verb, and it expresses a complete thought.]

SUBORDINATE CLAUSE that we had read about in the paper yesterday [This word group has a subject and a verb, and but it does not express a complete thought.]

A complex sentence contains only one independent clause. It also contains one or more subordinate clauses.

EXAMPLES A rainbow, **which contains seven colors,** is often seen in rain or fog. [This complex sentence has one independent clause, *A rainbow is often seen in rain or fog.* The subordinate clause, *which contains seven colors,* begins with a connecting word.]

When a rainbow forms, the bands of color **that you see** are always in the same order. [This complex sentence has one independent clause, *the bands of color are always in the same order.* Both subordinate clauses, *When a rainbow forms* and *that you see* begin with connecting words.]

EXERCISE A Draw one line under each independent clause and draw two lines under each subordinate clause in the following sentences. Then, circle the connecting word that begins the subordinate clause. Hint: Some sentences may contain more than one subordinate clause.

Example 1. Several students who arrived early for class talked with Mr. March until class began. [The two clauses that have a subject and a verb but do not express a complete thought are *who arrived early for class* and *until class began.* The words *who* and *until* are the connecting words.]

1. I will meet you at the game if I can get a ride with my brother. [Which part of the sentence has a subject and verb and expresses a complete thought? Which part of the sentence has a subject and verb but does not express a complete thought? What word begins the clause you underlined twice?]

2. While Mrs. Thompson was out sick, Mr. Harrison was our substitute teacher.

3. The story, which was written by Washington Irving, is about a headless horseman.

4. Although the house is clean, you should mow the backyard before the party starts.

5. The players followed the coach's orders without question because they respect her.

Compound-Complex Sentences

7d. A *compound-complex sentence* contains two or more independent clauses and at least one subordinate clause.

In the following examples, independent clauses are underlined once. Subordinate clauses are underlined twice.

> **EXAMPLES** I read the chapter, and then I answered the questions that were printed at the end. [This compound-complex sentence has two independent clauses and one subordinate clause.]
>
> If Trent will dust the furniture, Danny will sweep the floors and Luisa will make the beds. [This compound-complex sentence has two independent clauses and one subordinate clause.]

EXERCISE B Underline the independent clauses once and underline the subordinate clauses twice in the following sentences. Then, identify each of the following sentences by writing *CX* for *complex* or *CD-CX* for *compound-complex*. Write your answer on the line provided.

Example _CD-CX_ **1.** Whenever I get home from school, my dog Banjo meets me at the door, and my parrot sings a song to me. [The sentence is compound-complex because it has two independent clauses and one subordinate clause.]

_____ **6.** The first comedian was funny, but the second performer was the one that everyone will remember. [How many independent and subordinate clauses does this sentence have?]

_____ **7.** I have always been interested in astronomy, which is the study of planets and stars.

_____ **8.** The mustard that I put on my sandwich is extremely spicy, but I like it.

_____ **9.** The early American explorers whom I admire the most are William Clark and Meriwether Lewis.

_____ **10.** My lab partner, whose apartment is next to mine, is celebrating Kwanzaa this week.

Subject-Verb Agreement

8b. A verb should agree in number with its subject.

A subject and verb agree when they have the same number. When a word refers to one person, place, thing, or idea, it is *singular* in number. When a word refers to more than one person, place, thing, or idea, it is *plural* in number.

Singular Verbs

(1) Singular subjects take singular verbs.

>   S   V
> **EXAMPLES** The **swimmer looks** tired after practice. [The singular verb *looks* agrees
>
> with the singular subject *swimmer*.]
>   S   V
> My **sister** sometimes **helps** me with my homework. [The singular verb
>
> *helps* agrees with the singular subject *sister*.]
> S V
> **I think** about astronomy often. [The singular verb *think* agrees with the
>
> singular pronoun *I*.]

EXERCISE A Circle the verb form that agrees with the subject in each of the following sentences.

Example 1. This tent (*has*, *have*) a skylight. [The subject, *tent*, is singular, so the verb must be

singular, too.]

1. A removable cover (*protect, protects*) campers from rain. [What is the subject? Is the subject

singular or plural?]

2. My tent (*has, have*) windows that can be zipped shut.

3. A window (*allow, allows*) cool breezes to blow through the tent.

4. Fine netting (*keep, keeps*) out insects.

5. I (*enjoy, enjoys*) the sounds at night.

Plural Verbs

(2) Plural subjects take plural verbs.

>   S   V
> **EXAMPLES** **Crickets make** an interesting sound. [The plural verb *make* agrees with the
>
> plural subject *Crickets*.]
>   S   V
> Some **boys** in my class **own** unicycles. [The plural verb *own* agrees with
>
> the plural subject *boys*.]

GO ON

EXERCISE B Circle the verb form that agrees with the subject in each of the following sentences.

Example 1. The sounds outside at night (help, helps) me sleep. [The subject, *sounds,* is plural, so the verb must be plural, too.]

6. Most campers (*use, uses*) sleeping bags inside their tents. [What is the subject of the sentence? Is the subject singular or plural?]

7. Sleeping bags (*contains, contain*) insulation that retains heat.

8. Campers often (*needs, need*) pads under their sleeping bags.

9. Some pads (*are, is*) inflatable.

10. Pads (*makes, make*) the hard ground more comfortable for sleeping.

Agreement with Helping Verbs

A verb phrase is made up of a main verb and one or more helping verbs. The first helping verb in the verb phrase agrees with the subject.

> **EXAMPLES** **Dad is mowing** the lawn. [*Is mowing* is the verb phrase. The singular helping verb *is* agrees with the singular subject *Dad.*]
>
> Some **friends have joined** us for dinner. [*Have joined* is the verb phrase. The plural helping verb *have* agrees with the plural subject *friends.*]

REMINDER Even when the first helping verb comes before the subject, it should agree with the subject.

> **EXAMPLE** **Does Jake know** the answer to that question? [*Does know* is the verb phrase. The singular helping verb *Does* agrees with the singular subject *Jake.*]

EXERCISE C Circle the helping verb that agrees with the subject in each of the following sentences.

Example 1. Auditions for the school play (*is,* are) being held this afternoon. [The subject, *Auditions,* is plural, so the helping verb must be plural, too.]

11. Jane (*is, are*) sending a package to her mother in Vermont. [What is the subject of the sentence? Is the subject singular or plural?]

12. (*Is, Are*) the horses running across the field?

13. (*Has, Have*) the light in the kitchen gone out?

14. Rodney (*was, were*) enjoying his moment in the spotlight.

15. (*Does, Do*) the squirrels in your yard feed at night?

Subject-Verb Agreement: Compound Subjects

As you may remember, a subject tells who or what a sentence is about. Sometimes, two (or more) subjects form one *compound subject*.

S   S   S   V

EXAMPLE   **Kevin, Diane,** and **Mr. McBay teach** soccer at my summer camp. [*Kevin, Diane,* and *Mr. McBay* form a compound subject because all three people *teach.*]

Subjects Joined by *And*

8g.   Subjects joined by *and* usually take a plural verb.

V   S   S

EXAMPLE   **Are spring and fall** your favorite seasons? [*Spring* and *fall* are joined by *and.* The plural verb *are* agrees with the compound subject *spring and fall.*]

REMINDER The first helping verb in a verb phrase should agree with the subject.

EXAMPLE   **Buses and the subway have** long **been** inexpensive ways to get around the city. [The verb phrase is *have been.* The plural helping verb *have* agrees with the compound subject *Buses and the subway.*]

EXERCISE A Circle the verb in parentheses that agrees with the underlined compound subject in each of the following sentences.

Example 1. (*Has,* (*Have*)) you and your father finished your back-to-school shopping? [The subjects *you* and *father* are joined by *and,* so the helping verb must be plural.]

1. Department stores and sporting goods stores *(stocks, stock)* what we need. [Are the subjects joined by *and*?]

2. Before school starts, my mother and I *(shop, shops)* for school supplies.

3. Four pairs of socks and a vest *(costs, cost)* twenty-five dollars.

4. Pencils and erasers *(helps, help)* in all my subjects.

5. These jeans and this baseball cap *(is, are)* useful things to buy.

Subjects Joined by *Or* or *Nor*

8h.   Singular subjects joined by *or* or *nor* take a singular verb.

S   S   V

EXAMPLE   **Either Mike or Shelby sits** in that seat. [The singular verb *sits* agrees with the singular subject *Mike* and the singular subject *Shelby.*]

You will sometimes see these two word pairs: *either . . . or* and *neither . . . nor.*

GO ON ➡

EXERCISE B Circle the verb in parentheses that agrees with the underlined compound subject in each of the following sentences.

Example 1. *(Have, Has)* either the car or the van been washed? [The singular subjects *car* and *van* are joined by *or*, so the helping verb must be singular, too.]

6. Aunt Edna or my cousin Connie *(has, have)* the tickets to the musical. [Are the subjects singular? Are the subjects joined by *or* or *nor*?]

7. Either oregano or basil *(is, are)* necessary for this recipe.

8. *(Are, Is)* soup or salad included with the meal?

9. Either Carlton or his brother *(plan, plans)* to provide music for the party.

10. Neither the cat nor the dog *(like, likes)* to ride in the car.

8i. When a singular subject and a plural subject are joined by *or* or *nor*, the verb agrees with the subject nearer to the verb.

                 S   **S**   **V**

EXAMPLES A **sandwich or grapes make** a good snack. [The plural subject *grapes* is nearer to the verb *make*. The plural verb *make* agrees with the plural subject *grapes*.]

             S   **S**   **V**

Grapes or a sandwich makes a good snack. [The singular subject *sandwich* is nearer to the verb *makes*. The singular verb *makes* agrees with the singular subject *sandwich*.]

EXERCISE C Circle the verb in parentheses that agrees with the underlined compound subject in each of the following sentences.

Example 1. Mr. Davis or his students *(has, have)* decorated the bulletin board in the hallway. [The plural subject *students* is nearer to the verb, so the verb must be plural, too.]

11. Yesterday morning, either eggs or a bagel *(was, were)* what I ate first. [Is the subject that is nearer the verb singular or plural?]

12. *(Does, Do)* these newspapers or that phone book go in the recycling bin by the wall?

13. Neither food nor drinks *(is, are)* allowed in the computer lab!

14. According to the rules, either a short story or two poems *(count, counts)* as an entry in the writing contest.

15. Neither muscles nor the skull *(contribute, contributes)* to the human circulatory system.

Subject-Verb Agreement: Indefinite Pronouns

A pronoun that does not refer to a specific person, place, thing, or idea is called an *indefinite pronoun*. When an indefinite pronoun is used as a subject, make sure the verb agrees with the pronoun.

Singular Indefinite Pronouns

8d. Use a singular verb to agree with the following pronouns when they are used as subjects:

anybody	either	neither	one
anyone	everybody	nobody	somebody
anything	everyone	no one	someone
each	everything	nothing	something

> **EXAMPLES** **Somebody has** a good idea. [The singular verb *has* agrees with the singular subject *Somebody*.]
>
> Only **one** of the answers **is** correct. [The singular verb *is* agrees with the singular subject *one*.]

NOTE Many indefinite pronouns can also be used as adjectives. When these words are used as adjectives, they do not affect the number of the verb.

> **ADJECTIVE** **Each** tree has been trimmed. [The adjective *Each* modifies the noun *tree*. *Tree* is the subject of the sentence.]

EXERCISE A Circle the verb in parentheses that agrees with the subject in each of the following sentences. Each subject has been underlined for you.

Example 1. No one in my family ever (forgets), forget) a birthday. [The indefinite pronoun *No one* is always singular, so the verb should be singular, too.]

1. Everybody I know (*likes, like*) a sunny day. [Is the indefinite pronoun *Everybody* always singular?]

2. Anyone in need of help (*study, studies*) at the tutoring lab.

3. Each of the sparrows (*build, builds*) a nest.

4. Nothing (*has, have*) been done about the problem yet.

5. Everything (*seem, seems*) all right here.

Plural Indefinite Pronouns

8e. Use a plural verb to agree with the following pronouns when they are used as subjects:

both	few	many	several

> **EXAMPLE** **Several** of the athletes **won** gold medals. [The plural verb *won* agrees with the plural subject *Several*.]

GO ON

EXERCISE B Circle the verb in parentheses that agrees with the subject in each of the following sentences. Each subject has been underlined for you.

Example 1. <u>Many</u> of the instruments *(were) was)* tuned already. [The indefinite pronoun *Many* is always plural, so the verb should be plural, too.]

6. <u>Several</u> of the books *(have, has)* been returned to the library. [Is the indefinite pronoun *Several* always plural?]

7. *(Does, Do)* <u>both</u> of your sisters go to college?

8. By last week, a <u>few</u> of the birds *(was, were)* still looking for a place to nest.

9. <u>Many</u> of that author's stories *(are, is)* set in the same town.

10. Yesterday, <u>several</u> of the teachers *(were, was)* attending a conference.

Singular or Plural Indefinite Pronouns

8f. The following indefinite pronouns may be singular or plural, depending on how they are used in a sentence:

all	any	more	most	none	some

Look at the phrase that follows the indefinite pronoun. If the noun in that phrase is singular, the pronoun is singular, too. If the noun in that phrase in plural, the pronoun is plural, too.

EXAMPLES **All** of the **information is** helpful. [The subject *All* is singular because it refers to the singular *information*. The singular verb *is* agrees with the singular subject *All*.]

All of the **workers are** helpful. [The subject *All* is plural because it refers to the plural *workers*. The plural verb *are* agrees with the plural subject *All*.]

EXERCISE C Underline the subject in each of the following sentences. Then, circle the verb in parentheses that agrees with the subject.

Example 1. <u>Most</u> of the clouds *(holds, hold)* no rain. [The subject is *Most*. The noun in the phrase that follows the subject is *clouds*. The plural verb *hold* agrees with the plural subject.]

11. More of my attention *(is, are)* directed to the chalkboard than to my book. [What is the subject? Is the noun in the phrase that follows it singular or plural? Which verb agrees with the subject?]

12. Some of the farmers *(harvests, harvest)* the grain.

13. On the platter, all of the fresh biscuits *(is, are)* steaming.

14. *(Is, Are)* any of the orange juice left?

15. In our backyard, none of the trees still *(has, have)* their leaves.

Pronoun-Antecedent Agreement A

A pronoun is a word that takes the place of a noun or another pronoun. The word a pronoun replaces is called the pronoun's *antecedent*.

8p. A pronoun should agree in number with its antecedent.

Singular pronouns agree with singular antecedents, which may be nouns or other pronouns.

> **EXAMPLE** **Maria** showed **her** art project to the class. [The singular pronoun *her* agrees with its singular antecedent, the noun *Maria*.]

Some singular pronouns also have forms that tell the gender of the person or thing they name. Feminine pronouns (*she, her, hers, herself*) refer to females. Masculine pronouns (*he, him, his, himself*) refer to males. Neuter pronouns (*it, it, its, itself*) refer to things that are neither female nor male. Neuter pronouns also sometimes refer to animals.

> **EXAMPLES** My **stepmother** let me borrow **her** bat and glove. [The feminine pronoun *her* agrees with its feminine antecedent, the noun *stepmother*.]
>
> **Uncle Ed** has seen **his** favorite movie five times. [The masculine pronoun *his* agrees with its masculine antecedent, the noun *Uncle Ed*.]
>
> Stop the **cat** before **it** runs out the door! [The neuter pronoun *it* agrees with its neuter antecedent, the noun *cat*.]

EXERCISE A Read each sentence below, paying attention to the antecedent that has been underlined. Then, write an appropriate pronoun in each blank. Every pronoun you choose must agree in number and gender with its antecedent.

Examples 1. Will <u>Janette</u> read __*her*__ essay first? [The antecedent *Janette* is singular and feminine, so the pronoun must also be singular and feminine.]

2. The <u>book</u> with the red cover has lost __*its*__ spine. [The antecedent *book* is singular and neuter, so the pronoun must also be singular and neuter.]

1. Our Internet <u>connection</u> is running at _____ top speed today. [Is the antecedent singular or plural? Is the antecedent masculine, feminine, or neuter?]

2. We visited my <u>aunt</u> when _____ had surgery. [Is the antecedent singular or plural? Is the antecedent masculine, feminine, or neuter?]

3. When _____ finally blossomed, the <u>tomato plant</u> needed water.

4. Did <u>Kimberly</u> agree to bring _____ notes?

5. The thirsty <u>boy</u> got _____ a drink of cool water.

6. The stationary <u>bicycle</u> won't work if _____ power is turned off.

7. After mowing the lawn, <u>Earl</u> was thirsty, so _____ fixed a glass of lemonade.

8. A tall, blonde <u>woman</u> was looking for you, but _____ didn't leave a name.

GO ON

9. Can a <u>squirrel</u> jump from _____ nest to the ground?

10. <u>Ruben</u> has already finished _____ book report.

Plural pronouns agree in number with plural antecedents, which may be nouns or other pronouns.

> **EXAMPLES**   The **ants** rebuilt **their** colony after the rainstorm. [The plural pronoun *their* agrees with its plural antecedent, the noun *ants*.]
>
> Will **we** be making that important decision **ourselves**? [The plural pronoun *ourselves* agrees with its plural antecedent, the pronoun *we*.]

NOTE Plural pronouns do not show gender.

EXERCISE B Read each sentence below, paying attention to the antecedent that has been underlined. Then, write an appropriate pronoun in each blank. Make sure that each pronoun you choose agrees in number with its antecedent.

Examples 1. Both <u>coaches</u> were working on __*their*__ game plans. [The antecedent *coaches* is plural, so the pronoun must be plural, too.]

2. Are <u>potatoes</u> more nutritious when __*they*__ still have skins? [The antecedent *potatoes* is plural, so the pronoun must be plural, too.]

11. The <u>lilies</u> spread _____ sweet aroma through the house. [Is the antecedent singular or plural?]

12. Donny followed his favorite baseball <u>players</u> as _____ competed for the pennant. [Is the antecedent singular or plural?]

13. Four years ago, my <u>sisters</u> bought _____ a camera.

14. When the <u>children</u> need help, _____ will ask for it.

15. <u>Athletes</u> from around the country showed _____ skills.

16. When the <u>members</u> of the club ended the meeting, _____ locked the room and went home.

17. The <u>girls</u> left _____ shoes by the swings.

18. The <u>dogs</u> were loud when I arrived, but _____ quickly settled down.

19. The <u>boys</u> signed up for _____ favorite sports.

20. After _____ finish the assignment, the <u>students</u> may work on other projects.

Pronoun-Antecedent Agreement B

Singular Pronouns

| **8q.** | Use a singular pronoun to refer to the following pronouns:

anybody   either   neither   one
anyone   everybody   nobody   somebody
anything   everyone   no one   someone
each   everything   nothing   something

EXAMPLES   **Everyone** should bring **his or her** lunch. [*His or her* agrees in number with the antecedent *Everyone*, because both are singular. *His or her* agrees in gender, because *Everyone* may include males and females.]

Each of the boys brought **his** lunch. [The pronoun *his* agrees with the antecedent *Each* in number, because both are singular. *His* agrees in gender, too, because only males are included. The phrase *of the boys* makes the gender clear.]

EXERCISE A Read each sentence below, paying attention to the antecedent that has been underlined. Then, circle the pronoun in parentheses that agrees in number and gender with the antecedent.

Example 1. Each of my brothers enjoyed (*their,* (*his*)) year of seventh grade. [The antecedent *each* is always singular, so the pronoun must be singular, too.]

1. In the courtyard, everyone tried out (*his or her, their*) new locker combinations. [Is the antecedent *everyone* always singular?]

2. Nobody had forgotten (*his or her, their*) backpack.

3. Everything in the school had been cleaned until (*they, it*) sparkled.

4. The principal asked someone to bring (*their, his or her*) schedule card to the office.

5. My teacher had put everything in the classroom in (*its, their*) special place.

Plural Pronouns

| **8r.** | Use a plural pronoun to refer to the following pronouns:

both   few   many   several

TIP Plural pronouns do not show gender. When an antecedent is *both, few, many,* or *several,* the pronoun that refers to this word should be plural. Plural pronouns could refer to all males, all females, or a combination.

EXAMPLE   **Both** of the students have completed **their** assignments. [The plural pronoun *their* agrees with the plural antecedent *Both.*]

EXERCISE B Read each sentence below, paying attention to the antecedent that has been underlined. Then, circle the pronoun in parentheses that agrees in number with its antecedent.

Example 1. A <u>few</u> of the grapes have wilted; *((they)*, it)* are starting to look like raisins. [The indefinite pronoun *few* is always plural, so the pronoun that refers to it must be plural, too.]

6. <u>Many</u> of the model airplanes in Janie's room are interesting because *(it, they)* have movable parts. [Is the indefinite pronoun *Many* always plural?]

7. <u>Both</u> of the Olympic medals that the athlete had won were hanging in *(its, their)* display case.

8. We saw <u>several</u> of the monkeys in the zoo yesterday afternoon, and *(they, it)* were having snacks.

9. How <u>many</u> of the students chose blue as *(his or her, their)* favorite color?

10. At the museum, we saw a <u>few</u> of the paintings that were in *(its, their)* original frames.

Singular or Plural Pronouns

8s. The following pronouns may be singular or plural, depending on how they are used in a sentence:

all	any	more	most	none	some

Look at the phrase that follows the pronoun. If the noun in that phrase is singular, the pronoun is singular, too. If the noun in that phrase is plural, the pronoun is plural, too.

EXAMPLES **All** of the **test** was easy, wasn't **it**? [The pronoun *it* agrees with the antecedent *All*. The pronoun *All* is singular since it refers to one test.]

All of the **tests** were easy, weren't **they**? [The pronoun *they* agrees with the antecedent *All*. The pronoun *All* is plural since it refers to more than one test.]

EXERCISE C Look at the underlined antecedent in each of the following sentences. Then, circle the pronoun in parentheses that agrees in number with the antecedent.

Example 1. <u>All</u> of Mount Rushmore National Monument is made of granite, isn't *((it)*, they)*? [The pronoun *All* is singular because it refers to one monument, so the pronoun that refers to it must be singular, too.]

11. <u>Most</u> of the ice has already melted; *(it, they)* has been sitting in the sun for a few minutes. [Does *Most* refer to one thing or to many things?]

12. <u>All</u> of the library books sat neatly on *(its, their)* shelves.

13. <u>Some</u> of the baby birds could not yet fly, so *(they, it)* cried out for food.

14. <u>None</u> of the fossils could be identified until *(it, they)* were examined by the scientists.

15. Have you tried <u>any</u> of the salad yet, or are you waiting for someone else to try *(it, them)* first?

Regular and Irregular Verbs

All verbs have four principal parts, which are shown in the chart that follows.

Regular Verbs

9b. A *regular verb* forms its past and past participle by adding *–d* or *–ed* to the base form.

BASE FORM OF VERB	PRESENT PARTICIPLE (*–ING* FORM)	PAST (*–ED* FORM)	PAST PARTICIPLE (*–ED* FORM)
talk	[is] talking	talked	[have] talked
hop	[is] hopping	hopped	[have] hopped
direct	[is] directing	directed	[have] directed

TIP When people speak quickly, they sometimes sound as though they are dropping the *–d* or *–ed* ending, especially in words like *used, supposed,* and *prejudiced.* Keep in mind that, no matter how these words sound, they end in *–ed.*

NONSTANDARD   We were not suppose to know. [The *–ed* is missing from the past form.]

STANDARD   We were not **supposed** to know.

When you make a regular verb's past or past participle form, do not add unnecessary letters.

NONSTANDARD   I have already checkted the mail today. [The *t* that has been added after *check* is unnecessary. It should be removed.]

STANDARD   I have already **checked** the mail today.

EXERCISE A Fill in the blank in each sentence with the correct form of the regular verb. The verb you will use is given in parentheses after each sentence.

Example 1. Last year I ___*preferred*___ soccer. (*prefer*) [*Preferred* is the past tense form.]

1. Are you _____ to call your mother after school? (*suppose*) [What is the past tense form of the verb in parentheses?]

2. Has Shane been _____ autographs of famous soccer players? (*collect*)

3. Yesterday, the coach _____ us that we need to wear our uniforms. (*remind*)

4. I had already _____ my shinguards. (*remember*)

5. I _____ to think that soccer was a boys' game. (*use*)

Irregular Verbs

9c. An *irregular verb* forms its past and past participle in some way other than by adding *–d* or *–ed* to the base form.

Irregular verbs form their past and past participle in several ways.

(1) The verb's vowels may change.

BASE FORM	PRESENT PARTICIPLE	PAST	PAST PARTICIPLE
ring	ringing	rang	[have] rung

(2) The verb's consonants may change.

BASE FORM	PRESENT PARTICIPLE	PAST	PAST PARTICIPLE
ben**d**	bending	ben**t**	[have] ben**t**

TIP When you are not sure whether a verb is regular or irregular, do not guess. Look the verb up in a good dictionary. The dictionary will list all irregular forms of a verb.

EXERCISE B Underline the correct form of the irregular verb in each of the following sentences. Hint: You may want to review the list of irregular verbs in your textbook before doing this exercise.

Example 1. My big brother (<u>*grew*</u>, *growed*) a mustache. [The vowel *o* in *grow* changes to *e* in the past form *grew*.]

6. Robert (*gived*, *gave*) me a birthday card. [Does the vowel or consonant change in the past form?]

7. My grandparents' old lake cabin (*haved*, *had*) a fireplace.

8. Eric (*speaked*, *spoke*) to the class about the project.

9. Sue (*knew*, *knowed*) the address and phone number.

10. The door (*swung*, *swang*) open very quickly.

(3) The verb's vowels *and* consonants may change.

BASE FORM	PRESENT PARTICIPLE	PAST	PAST PARTICIPLE
th**ink**	thinking	th**ought**	[have] th**ought**

(4) The verb may make no changes at all.

BASE FORM	PRESENT PARTICIPLE	PAST	PAST PARTICIPLE
cost	costing	cost	[have] cost

EXERCISE C Underline the correct form of the irregular verb in each of the following sentences. Hint: You may want to review the list of irregular verbs in your textbook before doing this exercise.

Example 1. Have you ever (*catched*, <u>*caught*</u>) a fish? [Both the vowel and the final consonants of *catch* change in the past form *caught*.]

11. Where did you (*putted*, *put*) your jacket? [Does the past participle form change?]

12. The melon plants have (*frozen*, *freezed*) to their support posts.

13. Have you (*writed*, *written*) to the contest's sponsors?

14. I (*thought*, *thinked*) I already said that!

15. The rusted wheelbarrow (*stood*, *standed*) by the shed.

Verb Tense

The Six Tenses

9d. The *tense* of a verb indicates (or shows) when the verb's action takes place or state of being.

The time of an action or state of being can be **past, present,** or **future.** Every verb has six tenses. The six tenses show different ways of expressing time.

Here are three of the six tenses.

PRESENT The children **play.** [The present tense verb *play* shows an action that is happening.]

PRESENT PERFECT The children **have played.** [The present perfect tense verb *have played* shows an action that started to happen sometime before now. The action may continue into the present. Present perfect verbs begin with *has* or *have.*]

PAST The children **played.** [The past tense verb *played* shows an action that happened in the past.]

EXERCISE A Identify the tense of each underlined verb in the following sentences. Write *present, present perfect,* or *past* on the line provided.

Example *present perfect* **1.** The school bus has left from school. [*Has left* is the present perfect tense of the verb *leave.*]

_____ **1.** Cynthia bought her new shoes last weekend. [The verb shows an action that happened last week.]

_____ **2.** The trees in the park are green and full of leaves.

_____ **3.** Has Lori gone to the pool three days in a row?

_____ **4.** Anna thinks that Italian is a beautiful language.

_____ **5.** Timmy thanked his brother for his help.

Here are three more of the six tenses.

PAST PERFECT The children **had played.** [The past perfect tense verb *had played* shows an action that happened before a specific time in the past. Past perfect verbs begin with *had.*]

FUTURE The children **will play.** [The future tense verb *will play* shows an action that will happen in the future.]

FUTURE PERFECT The children **will have played.** [The future perfect tense verb *will have played* shows an action that will have happened before a specific time in the future.]

GO ON

EXERCISE B Identify the tense of each underlined verb in the following sentences. Write *past perfect*, *future*, or *future perfect* on the line provided.

Example ___*past perfect*___ **1.** Had Jane been there before? [*Had been* is the past perfect of *be*.]

_____ **6.** All of the books in that store will be on sale tomorrow. [The verb shows an action that will happen.]

_____ **7.** At the park, Kim said she had seen a lion only once before.

_____ **8.** The movie will have started by the time we arrive.

_____ **9.** Carla wondered whether Cameron had called.

_____ **10.** Will class begin promptly at 7:45 A.M.?

The Progressive Form

Each tense has an additional form called the ***progressive form.*** The progressive form expresses an action or state of being that keeps going on. In each tense, the progressive form of a verb consists of the appropriate form of *be* plus the verb's present participle.

REMINDER The present participle is the *–ing* form of the verb.

PRESENT PROGRESSIVE	The children **are playing.**
PAST PROGRESSIVE	The children **were playing.**
FUTURE PROGRESSIVE	The children **will be playing.**
PRESENT PERFECT PROGRESSIVE	The children **have been playing.**
PAST PERFECT PROGRESSIVE	The children **had been playing.**
FUTURE PERFECT PROGRESSIVE	The children **will have been playing.**

EXERCISE C Write the verb form indicated in parentheses on the line provided.

Example 1. Sunday ___*was*___ restful. (past tense of *be*) [*Was* is the past tense of the verb *be*.]

11. The plane _____ at 9:53 P.M. (past perfect tense of *depart*) [The past perfect is formed with *had*.]

12. We _____ to that park for years. (present perfect progressive form of *go*)

13. Jennifer _____ three books from the library. (past tense of *borrow*)

14. Alice _____ her English homework well. (present tense of *know*)

15. I _____ to the mountains with my family. (future progressive form of *go*)

Sit and Set, Raise and Rise, Lie and Lay

Sit and Set

The verb *sit* means "to be seated" or "to rest." *Sit* seldom takes an object.

REMINDER An object is a word that receives the action of a verb.

> **EXAMPLE** Please **sit** here and eat your lunch. [*Sit* means *be seated*. There is no object.]

The verb *set* usually means "to place (something somewhere)" or "to put (something somewhere)." *Set* usually takes an object.

> **EXAMPLE** I **am setting** the book on the table. [*Am setting* takes an object, *book*.]

TIP To choose between *sit* and *set*, try replacing the verb with a form of *put*. If the new sentence makes sense, then you will probably use a form of the verb *set*. If the new sentence does *not* make sense, then you will probably use a form of the verb *sit*.

> **EXAMPLES** Are you (*sitting* or *setting*) your backpack down by the wall? [Does *Are you putting your backpack down by the wall* make sense? Yes, so *setting* is the correct verb.]
>
> The rookie will (*sit* or *set*) on the bench for the game. [Does *The rookie will put on the bench for the game* make sense? No, so *sit* is the correct verb.]

EXERCISE A Underline the correct verb that completes each sentence.

Example 1. Please (<u>sit</u>, set) down at this desk. [*Sit* means *be seated* and has no object.]

1. Don't (*sit, set*) that hot pan on the table! [Does the verb have an object?]

2. The dog has been (*sitting, setting*) on the porch all morning.

3. When the bus moved, I (*set, sat*) down suddenly.

4. Will you please (*sit, set*) the plates on the table?

5. At 6:30 this morning, we were (*sitting, setting*) out the garage sale items.

Rise and Raise

The verb *rise* means "to move upward" or "to go up." *Rise* does not take an object.

> **EXAMPLES** My dog gets up when the sun **rises**. [*Rises* means *goes up* and does not take an object.]
>
> My dog got up when the sun **rose** this morning. [*Rose* means *went up* and does not take an object.]

The verb *raise* usually means "to lift something up." *Raise* usually takes an object.

> **EXAMPLES** **Are** you **raising** your voice so that I can hear you? [*Are raising* takes an object, *voice*.]
>
> Cedric **raised** his eyebrows. [*Raised* takes an object, *eyebrows*.]

EXERCISE B Underline the correct verb that completes each sentence.

Example 1. If you need help, (*rise*, <u>*raise*</u>) your hand. [*Raise* means *lift up* and takes an object, *hand.*]

6. The sun (*rises*, *raises*) later in the winter than in the summer. [Does the verb have an object?]

7. Which students (*rose*, *raised*) the flags today?

8. Antonio had (*raised*, *risen*) from his chair by the time I walked into the room.

9. The company might (*rise*, *raise*) the price of their product.

10. Your fever is (*raising*, *rising*); you need more rest.

Lie and *Lay*

The verb *lie* usually means "to recline," "to be in a place," or "to remain lying down." *Lie* does not take an object.

> **EXAMPLE** We **lay** down for a nap, and then the phone rang. [*Lay* means *reclined* and does not have an object.]

REMINDER *Lie* can also mean "to tell an untruth." Used in this way, *lie* still does not take an object. It is a regular verb that adds –*d* to make its past forms.

The verb *lay* usually means "to put (something) down." *Lay* usually takes an object.

> **EXAMPLE** Claire **laid** the coat on the bed. [*Laid* means *put* and takes an object, *coat.*]

TIP To choose between *lie* and *lay*, try replacing the verb with a form of *put*. If the new sentence makes sense, then you will probably use a form of the verb *lay*. If the sentence does not make sense, then you will probably use a form of the verb *lie*.

> **EXAMPLES** (*Lie* or *Lay*) down on your soft sleeping bag. [Does *Put down on your soft sleeping bag* make sense? No, so *lie* is the correct verb.]
> Nina will be (*lying* or *laying*) her purse on the floor. [Does *Nina will be putting her purse on the floor* make sense? Yes, so *laying* is the correct verb.]

EXERCISE C Underline the correct verb that completes each sentence.

Example 1. Has he (*laid*, <u>*lain*</u>) there for fifteen minutes already? [*Lain* means *reclined* and does not take an object.]

11. This picture frame is (*laying*, *lying*) on the floor in pieces. [Does the verb take an object?]

12. (*Lay*, *Lie*) that book on the top shelf.

13. Are we (*laying*, *lying*) the patio tile this weekend?

14. The weedy garden had (*lain*, *laid*) untouched for many years.

15. The cherry blossoms (*lay*, *laid*) like snow under the trees.

The Forms of Personal Pronouns

10a. *Case* is the form that a pronoun takes to show its relationship to other words in a sentence.

The Nominative Case

English has three cases for pronouns: the nominative case, the objective case, and the possessive case. The nominative case is used when a pronoun is the subject of a sentence. The nominative case pronouns are *I, you, he, she, it, we,* and *they.*

> **EXAMPLES** **He** enjoys playing soccer. [The nominative pronoun *He* is the subject.]
>
> **I** washed my mom's car. [The nominative pronoun *I* is the subject.]

EXERCISE A Underline all of the nominative case pronouns in the following sentences.

Example 1. Did <u>she</u> receive a call from a friend? [*She* is in the nominative case.]

1. We will show the project to the teacher. [What is the subject of the sentence?]

2. He can join the group today.

3. May I share that story with friends?

4. On Saturday they sometimes go to a movie.

5. Will she be at the museum, too?

The Objective Case

The objective case is used when the pronoun is a direct object, an indirect object, or an object of a preposition. The objective case pronouns are *me, you, him, her, it, us,* and *them.*

> **EXAMPLES** When you find the book, please bring **it** to **me**. [The pronouns *it* and *me* are in the objective case.]
>
> Jane's father gave **her** a winter coat. [The pronoun *her* is in the objective case.]

NOTE The pronouns *you* and *it* are the same in the nominative and objective cases.

EXERCISE B Underline all of the objective case pronouns in the following sentences.

Example 1. Please pass <u>me</u> the salsa. [The pronoun *me* is in the objective case.]

6. Felicia offered him one of the oranges. [Which word is a pronoun in the objective case?]

7. Have the students given the assignments to her?

8. David asked us about the awards ceremony.

9. Sarah shared a piece of fruit with them.

10. Marco, please bring me the dictionary on the table.

GO ON ▶

Developmental Language Skills

The Possessive Case

The possessive case is used when the pronoun shows possession or ownership of something. The possessive case pronouns are *my, mine, your, yours, his, her, hers, its, our, ours, their,* and *theirs.*

> **EXAMPLE** Is that **his** letter jacket? [The pronoun *his* shows that the letter jacket belongs to him.]

TIP Unlike nouns, pronouns do not need an apostrophe when used to show possession.

    INCORRECT Is that book hers', or is it his' book?

      CORRECT Is that book **hers,** or is it **his** book?

    INCORRECT I'll bring my book to the study session, and you can bring yours'.

      CORRECT I'll bring my book to the study session, and you can bring **yours.**

EXERCISE C Read each of the following sentences. Then, think of a possessive pronoun that completes the sentence's meaning. Write the pronoun on the line provided.

Example 1. Will Daniel bring __*his*__ basketball to the court? [The pronoun *his* shows possession

and is in the possessive case.]

11. The students checked _____ quiz grades. [Whose quiz grades were checked?]

12. Heidi claims that _____ cats are very smart.

13. We must keep _____ voices low in this museum.

14. The campers complained as rain leaked into _____ tents.

15. Is that maple tree losing _____ leaves yet?

The Nominative Case

10b. The *subject* of a verb should be in the nominative case.

> **EXAMPLES**   **He** pitched the tent while **we** prepared lunch. [*He* is the subject of the verb *pitched. We* is the subject of the verb *prepared.* Both pronouns are in the nominative case.]
>
> Did **they** donate the new uniforms? [The pronoun *they* is the subject of the verb *Did donate* and is in the nominative case.]
>
> Will **she** and **I** play on the varsity tennis team next year? [The pronouns *she* and *I* are the compound subject of the verb *will play.* Both pronouns are in the nominative case.]

REMINDER The nominative case personal pronouns are *I, you, he, she, it, we,* and *they.*

EXERCISE A Underline the appropriate pronoun or pair of pronouns in parentheses in each of the following sentences.

Examples 1. *(Her and me, She and I)* raked leaves in the yard. [The pronouns *She* and *I* are the subjects of the verb *raked* and are in the nominative case.]

2. After lunch *(he, him)* and Greg are going to play tennis. [The pronoun *he* is part of the complete subject, *he and Greg,* and is in the nominative case.]

1. *(He, Him)* and Chad collect baseball cards. [Is the pronoun used as the subject of a verb?]

2. *(We, Us)* waited in line for over an hour. [Is the pronoun used as the subject of a verb?]

3. *(They, Them)* are from Wyoming.

4. Last week *(she and I, her and me)* were winners at the county science fair.

5. *(Us, We)* jogged through the park together last Saturday.

6. Do *(her, she)* and Laura sit next to each other in health class?

7. Without my compass *(I, me)* would be lost.

8. *(He and I, Him and me)* like to bowl.

9. Are *(you, your)* going to the ballet Saturday night?

10. Every month *(him, he)* and Brad take aluminum cans to the recycling center.

10c. A *predicate nominative* should be in the nominative case.

A predicate nominative is a word or word group that is in the predicate and that identifies or refers to the subject of the verb. A pronoun used as a predicate nominative completes the meaning of a linking verb. (Common linking verbs are *am, are, is, was, were, be, been,* or *being.*)

> **EXAMPLES**   The strongest swimmer in that relay was **she.** [The pronoun *she* completes the meaning of the linking verb *was* and identifies the subject *swimmer.*]
>
> Were the only people in the theater **he** and **I**? [The pronouns *he* and *I* complete the meaning of the linking verb *were* and identify the subject *people. He* and *I* are a compound predicate nominative.]

TIP To choose the correct form of a pronoun used as a predicate nominative, reverse the order of the words in the sentence so that the subject and the predicate nominative change places. Try each pronoun by itself with the verb. Choose the pronoun that sounds right with the verb.

> **ORIGINAL**   The youngest contestant was *(him, he).*
>
> **REVERSED**   *(Him, He)* was the youngest contestant. [*He was* sounds right. *Him was* does not sound right.]
>
> **ANSWER**   The youngest contestant was **he.** [The correct pronoun is *he.*]

EXERCISE B Underline the appropriate pronoun or pair of pronouns in parentheses in each of the following sentences.

Example 1. The drum majors are (he and she, him and her). [The pronouns are used as the predicate nominative of the verb *are,* so the nominative case is correct.]

11. Wow! The contestants who scored the most points were *(us, we)!* [Which pronoun is in the nominative case?]

12. The drama club members who are performing are Jane, Bob, and *(she, her).*

13. My cousins are *(he and she, him and her).*

14. The runner who finished first was *(I, me).*

15. The cleanup crew should have been *(us and them, we and they).*

The Objective Case

10d. *Direct objects* and *indirect objects* of verbs should be in the objective case.

REMINDER The objective case personal pronouns are *me, you, him, her, it, us,* and *them.*

A *direct object* is a noun, pronoun, or word group that answers the question *Who (or What) receives the action of the verb?*

EXAMPLES Tanya recognized **him** as the owner of the van. [The pronoun *him* tells whom Tanya recognized. *Him* is in the objective case.]

Belinda picked some flowers and gave **them** to her mother. [The pronoun *them* tells what Belinda gave. *Them* is in the objective case.]

TIP To choose the correct pronoun in a compound object, try each form of the pronoun separately in the sentence.

EXAMPLE Melissa helped Todd and *(I, me)* with our homework. [Melissa helped *I* or Melissa helped *me*?]

ANSWER Melissa helped Todd and **me** with our homework. [The pronoun *me* tells whom Melissa helped. *Me* is in the objective case.]

EXERCISE A Underline the appropriate form of the pronoun or pair of pronouns in parentheses in each of the following sentences.

Example 1. Mr. Martino recommended *(I, me)* for the job. [The pronoun *me* tells whom Mr.

Martino recommended. *Me* is in the objective case.]

1. The loud thunderclap startled *(she, her).* [Whom did the thunderclap startle?]

2. Put the papers in an envelope and send *(they, them)* to Crystal.

3. Yesterday my dad took *(we, us)* to a good movie.

4. Will you see *(they, them)* this summer?

5. The magician entertained *(he, him)* and Darla.

An *indirect object* is a noun, pronoun, or word group that often appears in sentences containing direct objects. An indirect object tells *to whom* or *to what* or *for whom* or *for what* the action of the verb is done. An indirect object generally comes between an action verb and its direct object.

EXAMPLES Aunt Karen sent **me** a watch from Switzerland. [The pronoun *me* tells *to whom* Aunt Karen sent the watch. *Me* comes between the verb *sent* and the direct object *watch.*]

Tell **us** the story about your trip to China. [The pronoun *us* tells *to whom* the story is being told. *Us* comes between the verb *Tell* and the direct object *story.*]

Developmental Language Skills

EXERCISE B Underline the appropriate form of the pronoun or pair of pronouns in parentheses in each of the following sentences.

Example 1. Grandpa gave *(he and I, him and me)* some fruit. [The pronouns *him* and *me* tell to whom Grandpa gave some fruit. *Him* and *me* are in the objective case.]

6. Did you buy *(we, us)* some tickets? [For whom were the tickets bought?]

7. Didn't one of the cast members pass *(she, her)* a program?

8. The principal asked Mike and *(I, me)* to read the announcements.

9. The teacher handed *(we, us)* our exams as we walked into the room.

10. Larry's brother told *(he and I, him and me)* a joke.

10e. The *object of a preposition* should be in the objective case.

A noun or pronoun that follows a preposition is called the *object of a preposition.*

> **EXAMPLES** Butterflies were fluttering all around **us.** [The pronoun *us* is the object of the preposition *around. Us* is in the objective case.]
>
> Christie's mother sewed a blouse for **her.** [The pronoun *her* is the object of the preposition *for. Her* is in the objective case.]

EXERCISE C Underline the appropriate form of the pronoun or pair of pronouns in parentheses in each of the following sentences.

Example 1. The gift with the purple bow is from *(he and I, him and me).* [The pronouns *him* and *me* are the objects of the preposition *from. Him* and *me* are in the objective case.]

11. Please send a thank-you note to *(she, her).* [Which pronoun is the object of the preposition *to*?]

12. Near the campsite, a bear was moving toward *(he, him).* [Which pronoun is the object of the preposition *toward*?]

13. Do you think Daryl will leave without *(we, us)*?

14. That is a good picture of *(he, him).*

15. Is Nina riding with Aunt Susan and *(I, me)*?

16. These costumes are just right for Emilio and *(she, her).*

17. Who was sitting behind *(they, them)*?

18. Is the envelope addressed to David or to *(I, me)*?

19. Terrell sat between *(she and I, her and me)* in the cafeteria.

20. We received a phone call from *(they, them)* this morning.

Clear Reference

A pronoun should clearly refer to its antecedent. A pronoun takes the place of another word or word group. This word or word group is called the *antecedent* of the pronoun.

EXAMPLES   Mona left **her** book on the bus. [The pronoun *her* takes the place of *Mona.*

Mona is the antecedent of *her.*]

Before the plane took off, **it** was thoroughly inspected. [The pronoun *it*

takes the place of *plane. Plane* is the antecedent of *it.*]

EXERCISE A   Draw an arrow from the underlined pronoun in each of the following sentences to the pronoun's antecedent.

Examples 1. Ellisville has its own volunteer fire department. [The pronoun *its* takes the place of

Ellisville. Ellisville is the antecedent of *its.*]

2. Squirrels collect nuts and store them for the winter. [The pronoun *them* takes the

place of *nuts. Nuts* is the antecedent of *them.*]

1. Astronomy takes its name from the Greek word for *star.* [Which word does *its* stand for?]

2. Kyle wears sunscreen when he goes to the beach. [Which word does *he* stand for?]

3. Did Lee lay her keys on the table?

4. The CDs belong in their cases.

5. My brothers said they would like to run their own business.

6. How kind! Clifford bought a toy and gave it to his little sister!

7. Although stamps are inexpensive when new, their value increases over time.

8. Billboards often have catchy slogans on them.

9. Though Ariana enjoys the piano, isn't the violin her favorite instrument?

10. Donna said she hoped to see her friends over the weekend.

Avoid *unclear reference,* which occurs when any one of two or more words can be a pronoun's antecedent. Revise sentences with unclear reference to make each pronoun clearly refer to one antecedent.

UNCLEAR   Ed wrote Jeff a letter while he was at camp. [Who was at camp, Ed or Jeff?]

CLEAR   While Ed was at camp, **he** wrote Jeff a letter. [The pronoun *he* refers to Ed.]

CLEAR   While Jeff was at camp, Ed wrote **him** a letter. [The pronoun *him* refers to Jeff.]

Developmental Language Skills

EXERCISE B Revise each of the following sentences to eliminate unclear pronoun reference. Some sentences may be revised in more than one way. You need to give only one revision.

Examples 1. Even though the piano and the harp both have strings, they sound different.

Even though they both have strings, the piano and the harp sound different.

[In the revised sentence, the pronoun *they* clearly refers to *piano* and *harp*, not to *strings*.]

2. After school, Elizabeth and Jane went to the park with her sister.

After school, Elizabeth and her sister went to the park with Jane.

[The pronoun *her* clearly refers to *Elizabeth* in the second revised sentence.]

11. Mark called Adam before he left the house. [Who left the house?]

_____

12. Didn't Joe say that Ben had lost his keys? [Whose keys had Ben lost?]

_____

13. Maria passed Kelly her pen.

_____

14. The lamp has a new light bulb and a new switch, but it doesn't work.

_____

15. Joyce composed a song for the festival, and it was magnificent!

_____

16. Has Uncle Max asked his father if he could move the car?

_____

17. The umbrella is behind the door, but it won't open.

_____

18. Pedro told Andrew that he was just elected president of the class.

_____

19. The computer is too old for the new software, but I want to keep it anyway.

_____

20. Did Sarah hand Tanya her ticket?

_____

Forms of Modifiers

A *modifier* is a word, a phrase, or a clause that makes the meaning of a word or word group more specific. The two kinds of modifiers are *adjectives* and *adverbs*.

One-Word Modifiers

11a. *Adjectives* make the meanings of nouns and pronouns more specific.

> **EXAMPLES** Peacocks have **colorful** tail feathers. [The adjective *colorful* makes the noun *tail feathers* more specific. *Colorful* tells *what kind* of tail feathers.]
>
> Maurice prefers the **red** one. [The adjective *red* makes the pronoun *one* more specific. *Red* tells *which* one.]
>
> Is the sky **cloudy** this afternoon? [The adjective *cloudy* makes the noun *sky* more specific. *Cloudy* tells *what kind* of sky.]

11b. *Adverbs* make the meanings of verbs, adjectives, and other adverbs more specific.

> **EXAMPLES** The choir sang **softly**. [The adverb *softly* makes the verb *sang* more specific. *Softly* tells *how* the choir sang.]
>
> The new dress code is **quite** strict! [The adverb *quite* makes the adjective *strict* more specific. *Quite* tells *to what degree* the dress code is strict.]
>
> Isn't breakfast served **really** early at the ranch? [The adverb *really* makes the adverb *early* more specific. *Really* tells *how* early.]

EXERCISE A Underline the correct form of the modifier in parentheses.

Example 1. The cat rested *(lazy, lazily)* on its pillow. [The adverb *lazily* makes the verb *rested* more specific. *Lazily* tells *how* the cat rested.]

1. The doctor spoke *(kind, kindly)* to the patient. [How did the doctor speak?]

2. The gold coins are *(valuable, valuably)*.

3. Ahmed seems *(unusual, unusually)* happy today.

4. The meeting *(general, generally)* lasts one hour.

5. Claire wrote a *(sweet, sweetly)* letter to her grandfather.

Phrases Used as Modifiers

Like one-word modifiers, phrases can also be used as adjectives and adverbs.

> **EXAMPLES** **Flying through the air,** the eagle searched for prey. [The phrase *Flying through the air* acts as an adjective and makes the noun *eagle* more specific.]
>
> The public swimming pool closes **at dark.** [The phrase *at dark* acts as an adverb. *At dark* makes the meaning of the verb *closes* more specific.]

EXERCISE B Draw an arrow from each underlined phrase to the word it modifies.

Example 1. The contest ends in a few hours. [The phrase *in a few hours* is used as an adverb. It

makes the verb *ends* more specific.]

6. The basket of apples was full. [How is the phrase *of apples* used? What word does the phrase

make more specific?]

7. Beth came to my house after school.

8. The softball rolled under the bleachers.

9. The office opens at noon.

10. Wearing her bike helmet, she slowly pedaled out of the driveway.

Clauses Used as Modifiers

Like phrases, clauses can also be used as adjectives and adverbs.

EXAMPLES There is the man **whom we saw earlier.** [The clause *whom we saw earlier*
acts as an adjective. The clause makes the noun *man* more specific and
tells *which* man.]

Rebecca always locks the door **when she leaves the house.** [The clause
when she leaves the house acts as an adverb. The clause makes the verb
locks more specific and tells *when* Rebecca locks the door.]

EXERCISE C Draw an arrow from each underlined clause to the word it modifies. Remember: An
adjective clause modifies a noun or pronoun. An adverb clause modifies a verb, an adjective, or an
adverb.

Example 1. The CD player that I usually use is not working. [The clause *that I usually use* acts as

an adjective. It makes the noun *player* more specific.]

11. Barbara always calls us when she comes to town. [Which word does the clause *when she comes*

to town make more specific?]

12. Those shoes are the ones that she prefers.

13. Once the parade was over, everyone went back inside the building.

14. Jim is the student who writes short stories.

15. After we won the debate, we shook hands with the other team.

Degrees of Comparison

When adjectives and adverbs are used in comparisons, they take different forms. The form an adjective or adverb takes depends on how many things are being compared. The different forms of comparison are called *degrees of comparison.*

11c. The three degrees of comparison of modifiers are the *positive,* the *comparative,* and the *superlative.*

(1) The *positive degree* is used when at least one thing is being described.

> **EXAMPLE** That song is **slow.** [*Slow* is a positive-degree adjective. It describes one song.]

(2) The *comparative degree* is used when two things or groups of things are being compared.

> **EXAMPLE** That song is **slower** than this one. [*Slower* is a comparative-degree adverb. It compares one song to another.]

(3) The *superlative degree* is used when three or more things or groups of things are being compared.

> **EXAMPLE** That song is the **slowest** one on the CD. [*Slowest* is a superlative-degree adjective. It compares *That song* to all the other songs on the CD.]

EXERCISE A Identify the degree of the underlined modifier in each of the following sentences. Write *positive, comparative,* or *superlative* on the line provided.

Examples <u>*comparative*</u> **1.** These mountains look <u>higher</u> than those. [The comparative adjective *higher* compares two groups of mountains.]

<u>*superlative*</u> **2.** The <u>tastiest</u> treat Grandma makes is fruit salad. [The superlative adjective *tastiest* compares one treat to all other treats Grandma makes.]

_____ **1.** I checked my answers <u>well</u> before turning in the test. [Are things being described or compared?]

_____ **2.** This rocket is <u>more powerful</u> than that one. [How many things are being compared?]

_____ **3.** His eyes are the <u>greenest</u> eyes I have ever seen.

_____ **4.** I watched as the baby crawled <u>slowly</u> to the kitchen.

_____ **5.** Those shoes look <u>newer</u> than the ones you wore yesterday.

_____ **6.** Saxophone players often look <u>more intense</u> than other musicians.

_____ **7.** Marco asked whether the triangle was the <u>simplest</u> instrument in the band.

_____ **8.** The <u>most colorful</u> room in the house is my sister's bedroom.

_____ **9.** Alicia can make <u>stranger</u> noises with her voice than I can.

_____ **10.** I just lent the <u>funniest</u> book I have to my friend Jake.

Regular Comparison

Most one-syllable modifiers form the comparative degree by adding –er and the superlative degree by adding –est.

	POSITIVE	COMPARATIVE	SUPERLATIVE
ONE-SYLLABLE MODIFIER	hot	hot**ter**	hot**test**

Two-syllable modifiers form the comparative degree either by adding –er or by using *more*. They form the superlative degree either by adding –est or by using *most*. Some two-syllable modifiers can form comparisons either way.

	POSITIVE	COMPARATIVE	SUPERLATIVE
TWO-SYLLABLE MODIFIERS	often	**more** often	**most** often
	funny	funn**ier**	funn**iest**
	funny	**more** funny	**most** funny

Modifiers that have three or more syllables form the comparative degree by using *more*. They form the superlative degree by using *most*.

	POSITIVE	COMPARATIVE	SUPERLATIVE
THREE-SYLLABLE MODIFIER	interesting	**more** interesting	**most** interesting

REMINDER All modifiers form the decreasing comparative degree by using *less*. All modifiers form the decreasing superlative degree by using *least*.

	POSITIVE	COMPARATIVE	SUPERLATIVE
DECREASING COMPARISON	common	**less** common	**least** common

EXERCISE B Write the comparative and superlative degrees of the following modifiers.

Examples 1. tall _____ *taller* _____ _____ *tallest* _____

2. easily _____ *more easily* _____ _____ *most easily* _____

Positive	Comparative	Superlative
11. old	_____	_____
12. kindly	_____	_____
13. strong	_____	_____
14. neatly	_____	_____
15. challenging	_____	_____
16. soft	_____	_____
17. unusual	_____	_____
18. patiently	_____	_____
19. quiet	_____	_____
20. gently	_____	_____

Regular and Irregular Comparison

Regular Comparison

Most modifiers that have only one syllable form the comparative degree by adding *–er* and the superlative degree by adding *–est*.

EXAMPLES Mount Everest is **higher** than Mount Fuji. [*Higher* is a comparative-degree adjective.]

Mount Everest is the **highest** mountain in the world. [*Highest* is a superlative-degree adjective.]

Modifiers that have two syllables form the comparative degree by adding *–er* or by using *more*.

EXAMPLES The original version of the movie was **funnier** than the remake. [*Funnier* is a comparative-degree adjective.]

We finished our job **more quickly** than the other group. [*More quickly* is a comparative-degree adverb.]

Modifiers that have three or more syllables form the comparative degree by using *more* and the superlative degree by using *most*.

EXAMPLES The candidate spoke **more powerfully** at this rally than at the last. [*More powerfully* is a comparative-degree adverb.]

Ireland is the **most beautiful** country we visited. [*Most beautiful* is a superlative-degree adjective.]

EXERCISE A Complete each of the following sentences with the appropriate comparative or superlative form of the adjective or adverb given in italics.

Example 1. *favorite*   I don't like red. It is my _____least favorite_____ color of all. [*Least favorite* is a superlative-degree adjective. It compares how I feel about the color red and how I feel about all other colors.]

1. *long*   This year's Thanksgiving Day parade lasted _____ than last year's. [What is this year's parade being compared to?]

2. *large*   The convention center is the _____ building in the city.

3. *close*   Alaska is the U.S. state that is _____ to Russia.

4. *carefully*   Laura wraps her packages _____ than Anne wraps hers.

5. *fast*   This train is the _____ train in France.

GO ON

Developmental Language Skills

Irregular Comparison

The comparative and superlative degrees of some modifiers are irregular in form. Since these modifiers do not form their comparative and superlative in the regular way, you will have to memorize them.

POSITIVE	COMPARATIVE	SUPERLATIVE
bad	worse	worst
far	farther *or* further	farthest *or* furthest
good	better	best
well	better	best
many	more	most
much	more	most

EXERCISE B Complete each of the following sentences with the appropriate comparative or superlative form of the adjective or adverb given in italics.

Examples 1. *many* ____More____ people in my family watch football than in Tim's family. [*More* is the comparative degree of *many*. It compares the number of people in my family who watch football to the number in Tim's family.]

2. *good* The ____best____ vacation we ever had was the Colorado trip. [*Best* is the superlative degree of *good*. It compares one vacation with all others.]

6. *bad* Speaking in front of an audience is my _____ fear of all. [How many fears are being compared to each other?]

7. *well* Chris felt _____ today than she did yesterday. [What is being compared to how Chris felt today?]

8. *many* My uncle Ramon has _____ CDs than tapes.

9. *far* Amsterdam is _____ from Paris than Brussels is.

10. *good* A little sleep is _____ than none at all.

11. *many* Valerie gave _____ books to her brother than to her little sister.

12. *well* I work well with others, but I work _____ when I am alone.

13. *much* The _____ John spent on books was twenty-five dollars.

14. *bad* That performance was the _____ we have ever seen.

15. *far* The _____ Gilbert could run was three miles.

HOLT HANDBOOK | First Course

Placement of Modifiers A

Prepositional Phrases

11h. Place modifying words, phrases, and clauses as close as possible to the words they modify.

A **prepositional phrase** consists of a preposition, a noun or a pronoun called the *object of the preposition,* and any modifiers of that object.

> **EXAMPLES** The store **on the corner** ordered the parts. [The prepositional phrase *on the corner* modifies the noun *store.*]
>
> The detective searched all day **for clues.** [The prepositional phrase *for clues* modifies the verb *searched.*]

EXERCISE A Draw an arrow from the underlined prepositional phrase to the word it modifies.

Example 1. The parents looked at their newborn baby with love. [The prepositional phrase modifies the verb *looked.*]

1. Jim and Maria went to the Chinese restaurant near their house. [Which word does the prepositional phrase modify?]

2. Rosita read a book on the train.

3. The project for our social studies class took a week to finish.

4. We talked about the fair while we were at the park.

5. The tree with the red leaves has grown several feet this year.

Misplaced Modifiers

A modifier can either make your meaning clear for your reader, or it can cause confusion. A modifier that seems to modify the wrong word in a sentence is called a *misplaced modifier.*

A prepositional phrase used as an adjective should be placed directly after the word it modifies.

> **MISPLACED** That man is the president with the beard.
>
> **CLEAR** That man **with the beard** is the president. [The prepositional phrase modifies the noun *man* and is placed directly after the noun.]

GO ON

Developmental Language Skills

A prepositional phrase used as an adverb should be placed near the word it modifies.

MISPLACED	Amy said **on Friday** she would bring the book. [Will Amy bring the book on Friday, or did she make the statement on Friday? *On Friday* is a misplaced modifier.]
CLEAR	**On Friday** Amy said she would bring the book. [*On Friday* is closer to *said*. Friday is when she made the statement.]
	Amy said she would bring the book **on Friday**. [*On Friday* is closer to *would bring*. Friday is when she will bring the book.]

EXERCISE B Draw an arrow from each misplaced modifier to its correct location in the sentence. Hint: The misplaced modifiers have been underlined for you.

Examples 1. There is a bird at our feeder <u>with silver wings</u>. [The feeder does not have wings; the bird does. The modifier should be placed directly after *bird*.]

2. The band will play their new song at the concert <u>with funny lyrics</u>. [The concert does not have lyrics; the song does. The modifier should be placed directly after *song*.]

6. There is a suitcase under the bed <u>full of winter clothes</u>. [What is full of winter clothes?]

7. A sweat shirt is hanging in the closet <u>with a hood</u>. [What has a hood?]

8. Ted got the autograph of a swimmer who broke an Olympic record <u>at the mall</u>.

9. A dragon is a character in the new movie <u>with three heads</u>.

10. That magazine is on the coffee table <u>with several interesting articles</u>.

11. Father was given shirts by the dry cleaners <u>with stiffly starched collars</u>.

12. The grand piano is out of tune <u>in the concert hall</u>.

13. <u>Under the new microscopes</u>, will our class be looking at cells?

14. The bundle belongs in the recycling bin <u>of newspapers</u>.

15. The patient was transported from the accident scene <u>in a helicopter</u> to the hospital.

Placement of Modifiers B

Participial Phrases

A *participial phrase* consists of a present participle or a past participle and its modifiers and complements. A participial phrase is used as an adjective to modify a noun or a pronoun.

EXAMPLES **Studying late into the evening,** she fell asleep at her desk. [The participial phrase *Studying late into the evening* modifies the pronoun *she*.]

Leslie folded the **freshly washed** clothes and put them away. [The participial phrase *freshly washed* modifies the noun *clothes*.]

Like a prepositional phrase, a participial phrase should be placed as close as possible to the word it modifies. A participial phrase that is not placed near the noun or pronoun that it modifies is a *misplaced modifier*.

MISPLACED Brian prepared to take pictures loading the film into the camera. [Were the pictures loading the film?]

CLEAR **Loading the film into the camera,** Brian prepared to take pictures. [Brian was loading the film; therefore, the participial phrase should be placed close to *Brian*.]

EXERCISE A Draw an arrow from each misplaced modifier to its correct location in the sentence. Hint: The misplaced modifiers have been underlined for you.

Examples 1. The poster is a copy of a painting by Pablo Picasso hanging on my wall. [The poster is hanging on the wall, not Pablo Picasso.]

2. Shari jumped out of her seat startled by the noise. [Shari is startled, not the seat.]

1. Recently remodeled, the Chans relaxed in their family room. [What was recently remodeled?]

2. Alvin missed the awards ceremony arriving thirty minutes late. [Who arrived late?]

3. The fern needs water sitting on the windowsill.

4. Louise stumbled upon a piece of old wood searching for fossils.

5. Beautifully restored, we visited the Victorian mansion.

6. Carl dropped his wallet leaning over the balcony.

7. Pedro found some old coins searching for buried treasure.

8. The kite was just out of reach dangling from a tree branch.

9. Waving in the breeze, the race-car drivers could see the checkered flag.

10. The airplane was preparing to land circling overhead.

GO ON ▶

Developmental Language Skills

89

Adjective Clauses

An *adjective clause* modifies a noun or a pronoun. Most adjective clauses begin with pronouns such as *that, which, who, whom,* or *whose.* An adjective clause should generally be placed directly after the word it modifies. An adjective clause that is not placed near the noun or pronoun it modifies is a *misplaced modifier.*

> **MISPLACED** The movie star gave a newspaper interview who was visiting our town. [Was the interview visiting our town?]
>
> **CLEAR** The movie star **who was visiting our town** gave a newspaper interview.
>
> [The adjective clause modifies the noun *movie star.*]

EXERCISE B Draw an arrow from each misplaced modifier to its correct location in the sentence. Hint: The misplaced modifiers have been underlined for you.

Examples 1. The basketball player sprained his ankle who had been training for months. [The basketball player had been training. Therefore, the adjective clause should be next to *player.*]

2. Helmets are one requirement for the competition that protect in-line skaters. [Helmets protect skaters. Therefore, the adjective clause should be next to *Helmets.*]

11. The scooter was lying in the driveway that has a broken wheel. [What had a broken wheel?]

12. The explorers were from Norway who reached the South Pole. [Who reached the South Pole?]

13. My dog has a house in the backyard, whose name is Spunky.

14. The dishes are chipped that are in the cabinet.

15. The drama student practices in the hallway who has a lead role in *The Wizard of Oz.*

16. The swimming pool was finally filled with water, which had been empty since last summer.

17. Spanish is a language in many countries that is spoken around the world.

18. Our school song rang out over the loudspeaker, which was written by a former student.

19. Ming got a new sweater for her birthday that is red.

20. Sam helped me with my math assignment, whom I sit beside in class.

Glossary of Usage A

a, an   Use *a* before words that begin with a consonant sound. Use *an* before words that begin with a vowel sound. Keep in mind that the sound, not the actual letter, that a word begins with determines whether *a* or *an* should be used.

> **EXAMPLES**   This is **a** new book. [*New* begins with the consonant sound *n*.]
>
> What **an** interesting idea you have! [*Interesting* begins with a vowel sound.]
>
> We will attend **a** one-hour workshop. [*One* begins with the consonant sound *w*, even though the written word begins with a vowel.]

accept, except   *Accept* is a verb; it means "to receive." *Except* may be used as either a verb or a preposition. As a verb, *except* means "to excuse" or "to leave out." As a preposition, *except* means "excluding."

> **EXAMPLES**   I **accept** the nomination for president of the club. [You can replace *accept* with *receive*.]
>
> Students and senior citizens are **excepted** from paying the entrance fee. [You can replace *excepted* with *excused*.]
>
> No one **except** Julia thinks the dish tastes bad. [You can replace *except* with *excluding*.]

ain't   Do not use this nonstandard word in formal situations.

> **NONSTANDARD**   Carol ain't going to the movies this weekend.
>
> **STANDARD**   Carol **is not** going to the movies this weekend.

a lot   *A lot* should be written as two words. Never write *a lot* as one word.

> **EXAMPLE**   Rafael and Bruce don't have **a lot** of time today. [*A lot* is written as two words.]

EXERCISE A Underline the word or word group in parentheses that is correct according to formal, standard English.

Example 1. Please (<u>accept</u>, except) my apology. [You can replace *accept* with *receive*.]

1. Yesterday I saw (a, <u>an</u>) owl in the backyard. [Does the word following *a* or *an* begin with a vowel sound or a consonant sound?]

2. Do you have (<u>a lot</u>, alot) of work to do this weekend?

3. Everyone (accept, <u>except</u>) Selena has a passport.

4. We (ain't, <u>aren't</u>) finished yet with our homework.

5. Does Alex keep (<u>a lot</u>, alot) of pets in his bedroom?

GO ON

at Do not use *at* after *where*.

    NONSTANDARD I don't know where the cat is at.

    STANDARD I don't know where the cat **is.**

between, among Use *between* when referring to two individuals or items at a time. Use *among* when referring to a group rather than to separate individuals or items.

    EXAMPLES **Between** you and me, we can come up with a good plan. [*Between you and me* refers to two individuals, *you* and *me.*]

        Among the four of us, we can come up with a good plan. [*Among the four of us* refers to a group of four individuals.]

bring, take *Bring* means "to come carrying something." *Take* means "to go carrying something." Think of *bring* as related to *come (to), take* as related to *go (from).*

    EXAMPLES Please **bring** a dictionary to my house when you come.

        Please **take** a dictionary with you when you go to study at Jay's house.

could of Use *have*, not *of*, with the helping verb *could*. Write *could have*. Also use *have* after *ought to, should, would, might,* and *must.* When you speak, you may often pronounce the helping verb *have* as *of.* However, you should write it only as *have.*

    EXAMPLES Claire **could have/could've** [not *could of*] done that.

        Maybe you **should have/should've** [not *should of*] spoken to him sooner.

EXERCISE B Underline the word or word group in parentheses that is correct according to formal, standard English.

Example 1. I *(would of, would have)* never known if you hadn't told me. [*Have* is used with the helping verb *would.*]

6. The decision was made *(between, among)* all of the people involved. [Is the sentence referring to individuals or a group?]

7. Do you know where my new tennis shoes *(are at, are)*?

8. When you come back from the kitchen, please *(bring, take)* me that jar of pickles.

9. That *(must of, must have)* been Terry's voice on the answering machine.

10. Last week I *(could of, could have)* gone to the football game.

Glossary of Usage B

fewer, less   *Fewer* is used with plural words. *Less* is used with singular words. *Fewer* tells "how many"; *less* tells "how much."

EXAMPLES   Lisa is taking **fewer** courses than she did last semester. [*Courses* is plural, so *fewer* is used.]

Playing checkers requires **less** skill than playing chess. [*Skill* is singular, so *less* is used.]

good, well   *Good* is an adjective. Do not use *good* to modify a verb; use *well*, which can be used as an adverb.

EXAMPLES   Jasmine is my **good** friend. [*Good* is an adjective that tells "what kind" of friend.]

Did the band perform **well**? [*Well* is an adverb that tells "how" the band performed.]

NOTE Although it is usually an adverb, *well* is also used as an adjective to mean "healthy."

EXAMPLE   Rafael doesn't feel **well** today. [*Well* refers to Rafael's health.]

hisself, theirself, theirselves   These words are nonstandard English. Use *himself* and *themselves*.

NONSTANDARD   Did he complete the work by hisself?
STANDARD   Did he complete the work by **himself**?
NONSTANDARD   Alex and Ruben cleaned the garage theirselves.
STANDARD   Alex and Ruben cleaned the garage **themselves.**

EXERCISE A Underline the word in parentheses that is correct according to formal, standard English.

Examples 1. Shane has (*fewer*, <u>*less*</u>) time than I do. [*Time* is singular, so *less* is used.]

2. The customers helped (*theirselves*, <u>*themselves*</u>) to samples. [*Themselves* is standard.]

1. How (*good*, <u>*well*</u>) do you know Maria? [Which word should be used to modify the verb *do know?*]

2. Jim wanted to find out the truth for (*hisself*, <u>*himself*</u>). [Which is the standard word?]

3. The red box contains (<u>*fewer*</u>, *less*) items than the blue one.

4. Did you have a (<u>*good*</u>, *well*) time at the party?

5. Rochelle and Judy fixed the car (*theirself*, <u>*themselves*</u>).

6. The bottle holds (*fewer*, <u>*less*</u>) water than the canteen.

7. (<u>*Fewer*</u>, *Less*) fans than I expected attended the game.

8. Jennifer didn't feel (*good*, <u>*well*</u>) when she woke up this morning.

9. The band members wrote the music (*theirselves*, <u>*themselves*</u>).

10. It's a (<u>*good*</u>, *well*) idea to test smoke alarm batteries every six months.

how come In informal English, *how come* is often used instead of *why*. In formal English, *why* is preferred.

> **INFORMAL** How come you have to leave so early?
>
> **FORMAL** **Why** do you have to leave so early?

its, it's *Its* means "belonging to it." *It's* is a contraction of *it is* or *it has*.

> **EXAMPLES** The bird built **its** nest in the tree outside my window. [*Its* means "belonging to the bird."]
>
> **It's** my turn to water the plants. [*It's* is a contraction of *It is*.]
>
> **It's** been a long time since I have seen my grandmother. [*It's* is a contraction of *It has*.]

kind of, sort of In informal English, *kind of* and *sort of* are often used to mean "somewhat" or "rather." In formal English, *somewhat* or *rather* is preferred.

> **INFORMAL** Stacey was kind of disappointed when she heard the news.
>
> **FORMAL** Stacey was **rather** disappointed when she heard the news.

EXERCISE B Underline the word or word group in parentheses that is correct according to formal, standard English.

Examples 1. (*How come, Why do*) all of the students wear blue shirts on Fridays? [*Why* is

preferred in formal, standard English.]

2. (*Its, It's*) too hot this afternoon to go outside. [*It's* is a contraction of *It is*.]

11. We were (*kind of, rather*) surprised to discover armadillos in our backyard. [Which form is

preferred in formal English?]

12. Please explain (*how come, why*) the club should recruit more members. [Which form is preferred

in formal English?]

13. (*Its, It's*) been raining here all week.

14. No one knows (*how come, why*) Carol is worried today.

15. The obstacle course was (*sort of, somewhat*) challenging.

16. (*How come, Why do*) many fish swim in schools?

17. The car was missing one of (*its, it's*) hubcaps.

18. Didn't Monica seem (*kind of, rather*) cheerful in the meeting?

19. The art of paper folding is thought to have had (*its, it's*) origins in China.

20. (*Its, It's*) not too late to get tickets for tonight's concert.

Glossary of Usage C

than, then   *Than* is a word used in making comparisons. *Then* means "next" or "after that."

EXAMPLES   Lee is taller **than** her sister. [*Than* is used to make a comparison between Lee and her sister.]

Arthur finished his homework and **then** cleaned his room. [*Then* indicates that Arthur cleaned his room after he finished his homework.]

their, there, they're   *Their* is the possessive form of *they*. *Their* means "belonging to them." *There* is used to mean "at that place" or to begin a sentence. *They're* is a contraction of *they are*.

EXAMPLES   Many people leave **their** cars at home and ride the bus to work. [*Their* means "belonging to the people."]

Move the table over **there**. [*There* means "at that place."]

There is an information booth near the park entrance. [*There* begins the sentence.]

I suspect **they're** planning a surprise party for my birthday. [*They're* is a contraction of *they are*.]

them   *Them* should not be used as an adjective. Use *those*.

NONSTANDARD   Did Rosa buy them plants at the nursery down the street?

STANDARD   Did Rosa buy **those** plants at the nursery down the street?

this here, that there   The words *here* and *there* are not needed after *this* and *that*.

NONSTANDARD   This here basketball belongs to Tim.

STANDARD   **This** basketball belongs to Tim.

EXERCISE A   Underline the correct word or word group in parentheses according to formal, standard English.

Examples 1. Please pass (them, <u>those</u>) papers. [*Those* is used as an adjective and describes *papers*.]

2. Do (<u>their</u>, there) grandparents live in Minnesota? [*Their* indicates possession.]

1. The Eiffel Tower is much taller (than, then) the Statue of Liberty. [Which word is used to make comparisons?]

2. (Their, There) are two paintings above the couch. [Which word is used to begin a sentence?]

3. Tyrone, please shut the window and (than, then) close the blinds.

4. When does (their, there) flight leave?

5. How beautiful (them, those) shoes are!

6. Gabrielle likes volleyball more (than, then) she likes tennis.

7. Take (this here, this) jacket with you when you go outside.

8. Did the neighbors take (their, they're) dog with them on vacation?

9. *(That there, That)* book is a first edition of Ernest Hemingway's *A Farewell to Arms*.

10. While *(there, they're)* waiting for the tour bus, they can study a map of the city.

---

try and   In informal English, *try and* is often used for *try to*. In formal English, *try to* is preferred.

        INFORMAL   I will try and mail your package tomorrow.

        FORMAL   I will **try to** mail your package tomorrow.

whose, who's   *Whose* is used as the possessive form of *who*. It means "belonging to whom." *Whose* is also used as an interrogative pronoun—a pronoun that begins a question. *Who's* is a contraction of *who is* or *who has*.

        EXAMPLES   **Whose** watch is this? [*Whose* shows possession and means "belonging to whom."]

                        Whose is that? [*Whose* is an interrogative pronoun.]

                        Antonio has a sister **who's** a surgeon. [*Who's* is a contraction of *who is*.]

                        Who's finished the assignment? [*Who's* is a contraction of *who has*.]

your, you're   *Your* is the possessive form of *you*. It means "belonging to you." *You're* is the contraction of *you are*.

        EXAMPLES   May I take **your** picture? [*Your* modifies *picture* and shows possession.]

                        You're the first person I have seen today. [*You're* is a contraction of *you are*.]

EXERCISE B   Underline the correct word or word group in parentheses according to formal, standard English.

  Examples 1. *(Try and, Try to)* avoid driving in heavy traffic. [*Try to* is formal, standard English.]

         2. I can't tell *(whose, who's)* leading the race. [*Who's* is the contraction for *who is*.]

11. *(Your, You're)* calculator looks just like mine. [Which word means "belonging to you"?]

12. We should *(try and, try to)* find a shorter route to the city. [Which word group is formal, standard English?]

13. My aunt, *(whose, who's)* name is Elizabeth, sent me a postcard from Brazil.

14. *(Whose, Who's)* heard about the schedule change?

15. Gloria will *(try and, try to)* repair the damaged windshield.

16. *(Whose, Who's)* coming over for dinner this evening?

17. Please *(try and, try to)* arrive early for practice.

18. Return *(your, you're)* completed forms to the clerk.

19. *(Whose, Who's)* project was the best?

20. *(Your, You're)* the only one who knows how to run the machine.

First Words; Letter Salutations and Closings; The Pronoun *I*

First Words

13a. Capitalize the first word in every sentence.

> **EXAMPLE**   This sailboat belongs to my aunt Teresa. [*This* is the first word of the sentence.]

When a writer repeats someone else's exact words, the writer needs to put quotation marks at the beginning and the end of the other person's words. Putting quotation marks around someone else's words is called quoting. Any time you quote a sentence, begin the quoted sentence with a capital letter. You should do this even when the quoted sentence begins in the middle of a longer sentence.

> **EXAMPLES**   All of a sudden, Mark said, "**The** game will start in ten minutes." [*The* is capitalized because it is the first word of the sentence that is quoted.]
> "**We**'ll be on time if we hurry," said Karen. [*We'll* is the first word of the sentence that is quoted. *We'll* is also the first word of the longer sentence.]

EXERCISE A   Circle the letter that should be capitalized in each of the following sentences.

Examples 1. ⓣhe electricity went out during the thunderstorm. [The *t* in *the* should be capitalized because it is the first word of the sentence.]

2. Sometimes my sister Emma says, "ⓛet's go outside and play in the rain." [The *l* in *let's* should be capitalized because it is the first word in a quoted sentence.]

1. Rosie asked, "would you like a ride to school?" [Find the part of the sentence that repeats what somebody else said. Is the first word of the quoted sentence capitalized?]

2. why did he cut down that tree? [Is the first word of the sentence capitalized?]

3. please lock the door when you leave.

4. The coach blew her whistle and shouted, "take a break, everybody!"

5. "please tell me the price of those shoes," said Tom.

6. The dentist smiled and said, "have a seat in the chair."

7. "is Mrs. Lopez arriving tomorrow?" asked James.

8. last night we went to the movies with my cousins.

9. Mr. Fender said, "remember that your projects are due next Friday."

10. over the years, Ava has made many quilts for my family.

13b. Capitalize the first word in both the salutation and the closing of a letter.

The salutation is the short line at the top of a letter in which you greet the person you are writing. The closing is the short line at the bottom telling the person that the letter is about to end.

> **SALUTATIONS** **D**ear Mr. Edmonds: **M**y dear Clara,
>
> **CLOSINGS** **V**ery truly yours, **S**incerely,

NOTE Except for names and titles, the first word is the only word that is capitalized in a salutation or closing. In the salutation *My dear Clara*, *My* is capitalized because it is the first word of the salutation. *Clara* is capitalized because it is a person's name.

EXERCISE B Circle the letter that should be capitalized in each salutation or closing below.

Example 1. (t)o whom it may concern: [The *t* in *to* should be capitalized because it is the first letter of the salutation of a letter.]

11. dear Dr. Maldonado: [Is the first letter of this salutation capitalized?]

12. sincerely yours,

13. yours truly,

14. dear Aunt Christina,

15. my dearest Tom,

The Pronoun *I*

13c. Capitalize the pronoun *I.*

In English, the word *I* is always capitalized, even if it is not the first word of a sentence. Also capitalize *I* whenever you use it in a contraction, such as *I've* or *I'll* or *I'd.*

> **EXAMPLES** Did you hear that **I** won first place in the race?
>
> My mother says that **I've** always liked books.

EXERCISE C In each sentence or phrase below, circle the letter that should be capitalized.

Example 1. Do you think (I)'ll win first place in the contest? [The word *I* should always be capitalized.]

16. After dinner i will take the dog for a walk. [Is the word *I* capitalized?]

17. Should i come over to your house this afternoon?

18. "My guitar lesson is at four o'clock," i reminded her.

19. My brother and i have the same teacher for social studies.

20. Do you think i've run three miles yet?

Proper Nouns A

13d. Capitalize proper nouns.

A *proper noun* is the name of a particular person, place, thing, or idea. Proper nouns are capitalized. A *common noun* is the name of a type of person, place, thing, or idea. A common noun generally is not capitalized unless it begins a sentence or is part of a title.

PROPER NOUNS	Sandra King	Tillsdale Middle School	Peru
COMMON NOUNS	singer	middle school	country

PROPER NOUNS IN SENTENCES   My cousin **Lucinda** sings in the choir. [*Lucinda* names a specific person and is capitalized.]

The baseball team at **Williams High School** is excellent. [*Williams High School* names a specific place and is capitalized.]

The book has a photo of the **Statue of Liberty.** [*Statue of Liberty* names a specific thing and is capitalized.]

NOTE▶ Some proper nouns have more than one word. In these names, short prepositions (those of fewer than five letters) and articles (*a, an, the*) are generally not capitalized. Some common prepositions are *at, in, from, of, on, to,* and *with.*

EXAMPLES   Catherine the Great   *Pirates of Penzance*   *Romeo and Juliet*

EXERCISE A Circle the correctly capitalized word group in each pair below.

Example 1. Laura jackson   (Terence Cohen) [Both first names and last names should be

capitalized, so *Terence Cohen* is the correctly capitalized word group in this pair.]

1. canada   France

[Which word is a proper noun that is capitalized correctly?]

2. Raul Gonzales   Kevin robinson

3. new mexico   South Dakota

4. santa fe   San Francisco

5. Julie london   Carol Sloane

TIP▶ To tell whether a noun is common or proper, try placing *a, an,* or *the* in front of the noun. If you cannot, then the noun is probably a proper noun. It makes sense to say *a city,* so the word *city* is a common noun. It does not make sense to say *a Houston,* so *Houston* is a proper noun that should be capitalized.

GO ON ▶

EXERCISE B Write a proper noun that goes with each common noun below. Be sure to capitalize the proper nouns that you write. You can make up a name if you don't know one.

Example 1. cat _____ *Taffy* _____

6. city _____

7. friend _____

8. month _____

9. state _____

10. school _____

Capitalize the names of people and animals. When a name has initials, capitalize the initials.

PERSONS	Roberto Sanchez	Jeri Southern	J. P. Morgan
ANIMALS	Fluffy	Spot	Trigger

PROPER NOUNS IN SENTENCES The journalist **James L. Berkowitz** gave a speech. [*James L. Berkowitz* names a specific person. His name, including the middle initial, is capitalized.]

My pet bird **Coco** is a parakeet. [*Coco* names a specific animal and is capitalized.]

EXERCISE C Circle the correctly capitalized word group in each pair below.

Example 1. (our poodle Princess)   poodle princess [*Princess* is capitalized because it is the name of a specific poodle.]

11. katy Parker   Katy Parker

12. his dog scout   his dog Scout

13. Ida M. Brown   Ida m. Brown

14. a bird named Lola   a bird named lola

15. T. j. Warren   T. J. Warren

Proper Nouns B
Geographical Names

13d. Capitalize proper nouns.

Geographical names are proper nouns and should be capitalized. Geographical names include places such as countries, states, street names, and natural landmarks.

EXAMPLES	**A**ntarctica [continent]	**N**icaragua [country]
	California [state]	**S**an Diego [city]
	Pacific **O**cean [body of water]	**C**entury **B**oulevard [street]
	Mount **W**hitney [mountain]	**R**edwood **N**ational **P**ark [park]

NOTE When words like *north, south, eastern,* or *southwest* are used as the name of a region, they are capitalized. When you use these words to show a direction, don't capitalize them.

EXAMPLES	My father grew up in the **M**idwest. [region]
	That highway runs from **e**ast to **w**est. [directions]

EXERCISE A Circle any letter that should be capitalized in each of the following sentences.

Examples 1. The city of ⓣulsa, ⓞklahoma, always has a big parade on Independence Day. [The words *tulsa* and *oklahoma* name specific places and should be capitalized.]

2. According to the map, ⓢherman ⓢtreet is north of the highway. [The words *sherman* and *street* name a specific place and should be capitalized. The word *north* is lowercase because it is used here as a direction, not a region.]

1. One of the most beautiful cities in europe is paris. [Which words name specific places?]

2. Last year, I saw the atlantic ocean for the first time. [Which words name a specific place?]

3. Turn north on cartwright avenue.

4. My sister's husband is from panama.

5. Yellowstone national park has many hot springs and geysers.

6. Have you ever climbed mount shasta?

7. I like to read stories that are set in the southwest or the west.

8. Is boise the capital city of idaho?

9. I was really excited when our plane flew over the mississippi river.

10. The united states is not the only country in north america.

Organizations

The names of organizations, teams, institutions, and government bodies are proper nouns and should be capitalized.

> **EXAMPLES** **A**merican **L**ibrary **A**ssociation [organization]
>
> **H**amilton **H**igh **S**chool **H**ornets [team]
>
> **S**kyline **M**emorial **H**ospital [institution]
>
> **S**enate [government body]

NOTE Abbreviations of the names of organizations, institutions, and government bodies are often a set of capital letters.

> **EXAMPLES** **N**ational **A**eronautic and **S**pace **A**dministration   **NASA**
>
> **P**ublic **B**roadcasting **S**ystem   **PBS**

EXERCISE B Circle each letter that should be capitalized in each of the following sentences.

Examples 1. Where is the headquarters of the (I)nternational (O)lympic (C)ommittee? [The words *international, olympic,* and *committee* name a specific organization and should be capitalized.]

2. Many graduates of Martin Luther King (H)igh (S)chool go to college. [The words *high school* are part of the name of a specific institution and should be capitalized.]

11. Some doctors are members of the american medical association. [Which three words name a specific organization?]

12. My grandmother always watches the games of the Chicago cubs. [Which word names a specific team?]

13. The supreme court of the United States has nine judges.

14. Our school's team is the Fullmore falcons.

15. Did you watch the news on Nbc last night?

16. The Los Angeles city council makes the city's laws and approves the city's budget.

17. My uncle works in the emergency room at valley ridge children's hospital.

18. The north atlantic treaty organization (NATO) was established in 1949.

19. The quarterback of the Detroit lions will be speaking tonight at wayne state university.

20. I hope to become a member of the national honor society.

Proper Nouns C

Events, Dates, and Nationalities

13d. Capitalize proper nouns.

Be sure to capitalize the names of important events and periods in history. The names of other kinds of special events are also capitalized.

> **EXAMPLES** **W**ar of the **R**oses [historical event]
> **R**econstruction [historical period]
> **W**orld **S**eries [special event]

Always capitalize days of the week, months, and holidays. The names of the seasons of the year are not usually capitalized.

> **EXAMPLES** **S**unday, **T**uesday, **F**riday [days of the week]
> **M**ay, **A**ugust, **O**ctober [months]
> **N**ew **Y**ear's **D**ay [holiday]
> **s**pring, **w**inter, **a**utumn [seasons]

Words that name nationalities, races, or peoples begin with a capital letter.

> **EXAMPLES** **C**anadian [nationality]
> **C**aucasian [race]
> **C**herokee [people]

EXERCISE A Circle the correctly capitalized word group in each pair below.

Examples 1. (Stone Age)   U.S. Civil war

[All words in a compound noun that name a specific period in history should be

capitalized, so *Stone Age* is capitalized correctly.]

2. thursday   (Saturday)

[Words that name days of the week should be capitalized, so *Saturday* is capitalized

correctly.]

1. super bowl   Special Olympics

[Which word group names a specific event and is capitalized correctly?]

2. December 31, 2002   january 1, 2003

[Which word group names a specific date and is capitalized correctly?]

3. Independence day   Christmas

4. tuesday   Wednesday

5. european   Asian

GO ON ➡

6. spring   Summer

7. September   october

8. third week in november   Thanksgiving Day

9. world war II   Battle of Gettysburg

10. Italian   japanese

Businesses, Buildings, and Awards

The names of businesses and brand names are capitalized. Do not capitalize the name of a type of product.

     EXAMPLES   Kimberly-Clark Corporation [business name]

                       Kleenex [product brand name]

                       tissue [product type]

The names of buildings and other structures are capitalized. Do not capitalize the name of a type of building unless the word is part of the building's name. The names of monuments and memorials, which are often buildings or structures, are also capitalized. The names of special awards and prizes should begin with a capital letter.

     EXAMPLES   Kensington Palace [building name]

                       the king's palaces [type of building]

                       Washington Monument [monument]

                       Purple Heart [special award or prize]

NOTE Some proper nouns have more than one word. In these names, short prepositions (those of fewer than five letters) and articles (*a, an, the*) are generally not capitalized. Some common prepositions are *at, in, from, of, on, to,* and *with.*

EXERCISE B Circle any letter that should be capitalized in the following sentences.

Example 1. The Emmy Awards honor achievement in the television industry. [The words *emmy* and *awards* make a compound noun that names a specific award and should be capitalized.]

11. The scientist was honored to be nominated for a Nobel prize. [Which two words name a specific award?]

12. Does the book have a picture of buckingham palace?

13. My father eats kellogg's raisin bran cereal every morning.

14. My father has decided to sell our old Ford taurus.

15. The brooklyn bridge is a famous landmark.

Proper Adjectives; School Subjects and Course Names

Proper Adjectives

13e. Capitalize proper adjectives.

A proper adjective is an adjective formed from a proper noun. If the noun is always capitalized, the adjective should also be capitalized.

> **PROPER NOUNS**   China, Rome, Jefferson
> **PROPER ADJECTIVES**   Chinese paintings, Roman architecture, Jeffersonian democracy

EXERCISE A Each of the following word groups contains a proper adjective. Circle each letter that should be capitalized.

Examples 1. a Ⓢpanish guitar [The adjective *spanish* is formed from the proper noun *Spain*. The *s* in *spanish* should be capitalized.]

2. an Ⓔlizabethan poet [The adjective *elizabethan* is formed from the proper noun *Elizabeth*. The *e* in *elizabethan* should be capitalized.]

1. the roman calendar [Which word is an adjective formed from the proper noun Rome?]

2. a shakespearean play [Which word is an adjective formed from a proper noun?]

3. a british accent

4. a greek restaurant

5. the chinese ambassador

6. an irish folk tale

7. the martian atmosphere

8. american history

9. victorian fashions

10. a mexican city

School Subjects

13f. Do not capitalize the names of school subjects, except names of language classes and course names followed by numerals.

> **EXAMPLES**   band, keyboarding [subjects or classes]
> Concert Band II [course name with numeral]
> French, English [language classes]

GO ON

for **CHAPTER 13: CAPITAL LETTERS**   *pages 276-77* *continued*

EXERCISE B Circle any letter that should be capitalized in the following sentences. Draw a slash (/) through any letter that is capitalized but should not be.

Examples 1. My M̷ath teacher also teaches ⒻFrench courses. [The word *Math* names a school subject and is not followed by a numeral. *Math* should not be capitalized. The word *French* names a language and should be capitalized.]

     2. Are you in the C̷hoir or in ⒷBand II this year? [The word *Choir* names a school subject and is not followed by a numeral. *Choir* should not be capitalized. The word *band* is followed by a numeral and should be capitalized.]

11. We are studying the history of California in my social studies I class. [Which words name a class? Is the subject a language? Is the name of the class followed by a numeral?]

12. For one of my electives, I have chosen Art History. [Which words name a school subject? Is the subject a language? Is the name of the class followed by a numeral?]

13. At our school, you can study spanish, french, german, or latin.

14. You have to complete biology I before you can take a Chemistry class.

15. The language arts 201 class will meet in the cafeteria this morning.

16. Will you sit next to me in Algebra next year?

17. Jeff takes a Physical Education course every semester.

18. My Geography teacher is originally from Korea.

19. In Music appreciation 101 we have been listening to folk songs.

20. The students in journalism II design the school's yearbook.

Titles of Persons and Creative Works

13g.   Capitalize titles.

Titles of Persons

Always capitalize the title of a person when the title comes before the person's name. Even if the title is abbreviated, capitalize it.

> **EXAMPLES**   I read a biography of **G**eneral Colin Powell. [The title **General** comes before the person's name.]
>
> When did he become a **g**eneral? [The word *general* does not come before a person's name.]
>
> This is the office of **D**r. Sara H. Braun. [The title *Dr.*, which is the abbreviation for *Doctor*, comes before the person's name.]
>
> She always wanted to become a **d**octor. [The word *doctor* does not come before a person's name.]

EXERCISE A Circle each letter that should be capitalized in the following sentences and phrases. Draw a slash through each letter that is capitalized but should be lowercase.

Example 1. Mr. and ⟨m⟩rs. Smith live across the street. [Both *Mr.* and *Mrs.* come before *Smith*, so they both should be capitalized.]

1. Our class talked to Miguel Martin, a well-known Doctor. [Which word is a title that does not come before a person's name?]

2. Have you read professor Albright's latest book?

3. That letter was addressed to ms. Fellows, our history teacher.

4. How long does it take to get the rank of Sergeant?

5. When she was downtown yesterday, Kim saw mayor Watson.

> A word that shows a family relationship is capitalized when the word comes before the person's name or is used in place of the person's name.
>
> > **EXAMPLES**   Please show this letter to **U**ncle Dave. [*Uncle* comes before the person's name.]
> >
> > I asked **M**om to drive us to the movies. [*Mom* is used in place of the name of the person.]
>
> However, do not capitalize a word showing a family relationship when a possessive comes before the word.
>
> > **EXAMPLE**   My **a**unt Alice lives in Oregon. [The word *aunt* is preceded by a possessive, so *aunt* is not capitalized.]

GO ON ➡

EXERCISE B Circle each letter that should be capitalized in the following sentences and phrases. Draw a slash through each letter that is capitalized but should be lowercase.

Example 1. Let me introduce you to@unt Clara. [The word *aunt* comes before the name *Clara* and is not preceded by a possessive, so it should be capitalized.]

6. The photo of grandma and grandpa is sitting on the coffee table. [Which two words are used in place of someone's name?]

7. Ask dad if he will drive us to the store.

8. I will write a letter to uncle Mike.

9. Did your Brother Jason replace the bike tire yet?

10. Please give a warm welcome to my Cousin Serena.

Titles of Creative Works

Whenever you write the title of a book, a poem, or any other creative work, be sure to capitalize the first word, the last word, and all other important words. Capitalize these words in subtitles, too. Do not capitalize an article (*a, an,* or *the*) or a short preposition (such as *of, in,* or *with*) unless the article or preposition is the first or last word in the title or subtitle.

EXAMPLES *The Once and Future King* [book] *Mr. Smith Goes to Washington* [movie]
Our Town [play] *The Washington Post* [newspaper]
American Gothic [painting] *Peanuts* [comic strip]
"The Star-Spangled Banner" [song] Treaty of Versailles
"The Second Coming" [poem] [historical document]
Nova [television series]

EXERCISE C Circle any letter that should be capitalized in the following phrases.

Example 1. John Steinbeck's novel *The grapes of wrath* [The words *grapes* and *wrath* are important words in the title and should be capitalized. The word *of* is a short preposition and should not be capitalized.]

11. the Beatles song "a day in the life" [Which two words are important words in the title? Which word is an article that is the first word in the title?]

12. *Reader's digest,* my grandmother's favorite magazine

13. one of the characters in the comic strip *jump start*

14. a story on the television program *60 minutes*

15. "the fall of the house of usher," a story by Edgar Allan Poe

                                       HOLT HANDBOOK | First Course

Commas with Compound Sentences

14h.

> **REMINDER** An *independent clause* is a group of words that a) has a subject and a verb and b) can stand alone as a sentence.
>
> **EXAMPLE**   Lupe fed her new pony. [*Lupe* is the subject, and *fed* is the verb. The clause can stand alone as a sentence.]
>
> The subject and the verb of an independent clause may be compound.
>
> **EXAMPLE**   Lupe and her brother fed and brushed their new pony. [*Lupe* and *brother* are the compound subject. *Fed* and *brushed* are the compound verb. The clause can stand alone as a sentence.]
>
> A *compound sentence* is made of two or more independent clauses.
>
> **EXAMPLES**   Linda collected canned food for her school's food drive**, and** she and her mother volunteered at the food bank. [The compound sentence consists of two independent clauses joined by a comma and the word *and*.]
>
> Uncle Geraldo may move to San Diego**, or** he may move to Chicago. [The compound sentence consists of two independent clauses joined by a comma and the word *or*.]
>
> The carpenter and his assistant sanded and painted the wood**, but** they did not install the window. [The compound sentence consists of two independent clauses joined by a comma and the word *but*.]

EXERCISE A   For each of the following compound sentences, add commas where they are needed.

Examples 1. Joe High Eagle was born on an Apache reservation, and he grew up there in the White Mountains of Arizona. [The first independent clause, *Joe High Eagle was born on an Apache reservation,* and the second independent clause, *he grew up there in the White Mountains of Arizona,* are joined by a comma and the word *and*.]

  2. Joe has many fond memories of his childhood, for he was very active and had many friends. [The first independent clause, *Joe has many fond memories of his childhood,* and the second independent clause, *he was very active and had many friends,* are joined by a comma and the word *for*.]

1. Don Foley also grew up on the reservation but he was not an Apache. [Where does the first independent clause end and the second begin? What word is being used to combine the two clauses? Place the comma before that word.]

GO ON ➡

2. Don's family ran the trading post so they lived on the reservation. [Where does the first independent clause end and the second begin? What word is being used to combine the two clauses? Place the comma before that word.]

3. Joe and Don lived next door to each other and they were almost like brothers.

4. They spent most of their time outdoors and they loved the freedom.

5. They would hike in the mountains or they would swim and fish in the streams.

6. Joe's father was a tribe elder and he often accompanied the boys on their adventures.

7. Joe's father was also an excellent tracker so he and the boys would study animal tracks along the trails.

8. They would camp under the stars and Joe's father would tell stories.

9. The boys would look up at the stars for hours or they would just close their eyes and listen to the coyotes in the distance.

10. Sometimes a noise would startle them but they always felt safe with Joe's father around.

EXERCISE B For each of the following compound sentences, add commas where they are needed.

Example 1. Don's father found a job in Phoenix, so the family moved. [The first independent clause, *Don's father found a job in Phoenix,* and the second independent clause, *the family moved,* are joined by a comma and the word *so.*]

11. The trading post was handed over to the tribe and everyone in Don's family said goodbye to their friends. [Where does the first independent clause end and the second begin? What word is being used to combine the two clauses?]

12. There were no hard feelings and there were no regrets.

13. Don liked his new home and made new friends but he missed Joe and the White Mountains.

14. The two boys wrote each other often and sometimes Don would visit the reservation in the summer.

15. Don and Joe have kept in touch over the years so they are still good friends.

HOLT HANDBOOK | First Course

Commas with Sentence Interrupters and Introductory Elements

Sentence Interrupters

14i. Use commas to set off an expression that interrupts a sentence.

Interrupters often add extra information to a sentence. Some interrupters come at the beginning of the sentence; some come in the middle; and some come at the end. Interrupters are separated from the rest of the sentence with commas.

> **EXAMPLES** **Ginny,** that was a great jump shot. [The word *Ginny* interrupts the rest of the sentence, so it is followed by a comma.]
>
> Shaun, **humming a cheerful tune,** walked through the park. [The added information *humming a cheerful tune* interrupts the sentence. A comma is placed before and after the interrupter.]
>
> I read *Call of the Wild,* **which is a wonderful book,** in my English class. [The added information *which is a wonderful book* interrupts the sentence. A comma is placed before and after the interrupter.]
>
> My grandmother lives near Louisiana's capital, **Baton Rouge.** [The added information *Baton Rouge* interrupts the sentence, so it is set off by a comma.]
>
> We pleaded to go home early, **of course.** [The interrupter *of course* is set off by a comma.]

EXERCISE A The following sentences contain sentence interrupters. Punctuate the interrupters correctly by adding the necessary commas.

Examples 1. The artist signed only her first name, Sarah. [The added information *Sarah* interrupts the sentence, so it is set off by a comma.]

2. The politician, hoping for more votes, kissed the baby. [The added information *hoping for more votes* interrupts the sentence, so it is set off by commas.]

1. Tara who has a wonderful voice will sing a solo. [What extra information about Tara interrupts the sentence?]

2. Please read the next paragraph Patrick. [What word interrupts the sentence?]

3. In my opinion the best drawing is the one of the black horse.

4. Mr. Schneider my biology teacher is the sponsor of the Science Club.

5. Eduardo the captain of the basketball team scored the winning point.

6. Kimi that was your best time for this event.

7. The horned lizard now a threatened species used to be a common sight.

8. I would rather attend the school play to tell the truth.

9. The auto mechanic keeping up to date with technology has a new computer.

10. William Blake my favorite poet beautifully illustrated his poems.

Introductory Elements

14j. | Use a comma after certain introductory elements.

Introductory elements are always at the beginning of a sentence, and they are set off from the rest of the sentence by a comma.

> EXAMPLES **No,** I don't want to go ice skating tonight. [The introductory word *No* is followed by a comma.]
>
> **In the yard across the street,** the dog sat on the porch. [The introductory phrase *In the yard across the street* is followed by a comma.]
>
> **Before she begins packing for a trip,** my mother always makes a checklist. [The introductory clause *Before she begins packing for a trip* is followed by a comma.]

EXERCISE B The following sentences contain introductory elements. Punctuate the sentences correctly by adding necessary commas.

Examples 1. In the bottom of the ninth inning, Billy hit a home run. [The introductory material, *In the bottom of the ninth inning,* is set off from the rest of the sentence by a comma.]

2. When you finish your homework, you may play basketball. [The introductory material, *When you finish your homework,* is set off from the rest of the sentence by a comma.]

11. Yes the test will include an essay question. [Where does the introductory material end?]

12. In front of the whole seventh grade Frances gave her speech. [Where does the introductory material end?]

13. Why that's wonderful news!

14. Looking for her favorite toy Joel's little sister wandered from room to room.

15. During the Fall Carnival at our school Ms. Martin wore a clown suit.

16. After I finish my chores can I play tennis with Sue?

17. Practicing their lines with one another Marco and Chen waited for their turn to audition.

18. Pleased with his grade Nigel was glad that he had asked the teacher for help.

19. Before you leave for the swim meet could you take out the trash?

20. Yes you can help me shell the peas.

 HOLT HANDBOOK | First Course

Semicolons and Colons

Semicolons

14l. Use a semicolon between independent clauses if they are not joined by *and, but, for, nor, or, so,* or *yet.*

> **EXAMPLE**   Gabriella participates in many school-sponsored activities; she plays on the volleyball team and mentors. [The two independent clauses are joined by a semicolon.]

Independent clauses should be joined by a semicolon only if they are closely related. If the clauses are not closely related, then they should remain separate sentences.

> **EXAMPLES**   Patrick is my dog; Bardo is my cat. [These two sentences can be joined with a semicolon because they are closely related. Both sentences identify pets.]
>
> Patrick is my dog. My cat Bardo has fleas. [These two sentences should not be joined with a semicolon. Even though they both mention pets, the sentences are not about the same thing. One sentence identifies Patrick; the other says that Bardo has fleas.]

EXERCISE A   For each of the following sentences, decide if the independent clauses are closely related and can be joined by a semicolon. If they can be joined by a semicolon, write *semicolon* on the line provided. If the clauses should not be joined by a semicolon, write *C* on the line.

Example   _____*semicolon*_____   **1.** The players went inside the field house. The fans returned to their homes. [The two sentences are closely related.]

_____   **1.** Roses are red. Violets are blue. [Are the sentences closely related? Do they provide the same kind of information?]

_____   **2.** Jo Ann likes science fiction. Pierre lost his book.

_____   **3.** Sir Isaac Newton discovered gravity. Marie Curie discovered radium.

_____   **4.** Gerald likes scary movies. La Shanda prefers musicals.

_____   **5.** Foster likes mythology. Neptune is the Roman god of the sea.

Colons

14n. Use a colon before a list of items, especially after expressions such as *the following* or *as follows.*

> **EXAMPLES**   Paula has four items in her grocery basket: milk, bread, pears, and apples. [The colon introduces a list of items in the basket.]
>
> The members of the team are as follows: Joleene, Cathy, and Karen. [The expression *as follows* plus the colon introduces a list of the team members.]

EXERCISE B Insert colons where they are needed in the following sentences.

Example 1. For the field trip, please bring the following: a bag lunch, a jacket, and comfortable shoes. [The expression _the following_ plus the colon introduces the list of items needed for the field trip.]

6. Teams will enter the auditorium as follows the Tigers, the Northstars, the Blackshirts, and the Eagles. [What phrase signals the beginning of a list? Use a colon to separate the list from the rest of the sentence.]

7. I have family in several states Texas, Wyoming, Florida, and Rhode Island.

8. Jill shopped for new clothes a sweater, some socks, and a pair of jeans.

9. Chao's garden contains a variety of flowers roses, petunias, irises, and lilacs.

10. Will you bring the following items a map, a compass, and binoculars?

14o. Use a colon between the hour and the minute.

    EXAMPLES 2:30 P.M.   9:00 in the morning

14p. Use a colon after the salutation of a business letter.

    EXAMPLES Dear Senator Evans: To Whom It May Concern:

14q. Use a colon between chapter and verse in Biblical references and between all titles and subtitles.

    EXAMPLES 1 John 1:9 [_1 John 1_ is the chapter. _9_ is the verse.]

    Making Healthy Choices: Staples of a Low-Fat Diet [_Making Healthy Choices_ is the title. _Staples of a Low-Fat Diet_ is the subtitle.]

EXERCISE C Insert colons where they are needed in the following items.

Example 1. Dear Dr. Metcalf: [_Dear Dr. Metcalf_ is the salutation of a business letter, so it is followed by a colon.]

11. The job interview is at 9 30 A.M. [What does the colon separate in expressions of time?]

12. I read about the battle between David and Goliath in I Samuel 17 4–58.

13. Dear Sir or Madam

14. The next bus is due at 10 45 this evening.

15. The title of my sister's scrapbook is Lasting Memories My Senior Year.

Underlining (Italics)

15a. Use underlining (italics) for titles and subtitles of books, plays, periodicals, films, television series, works of art, and long musical works.

When you write the title of a book, a play, a movie, a magazine, a newspaper, or some other major creative work, underline the entire title. A typesetter would set underlined words in *italics,* letters that lean to the right. If you use a computer, you can probably set these titles in italics yourself. Do not underline titles that you have set in italics. Use underlining or italics, but not both.

ITALICIZED	*Harvey* [play]	*The Four Seasons* [long musical work]
	North by Northwest [movie]	*The Atlantic Monthly* [magazine]
	In the Shadow of a Rainbow: The True Story of a Friendship Between Man and Wolf [book]	*Frontline* [television series]
UNDERLINED	<u>Harvey</u>	<u>The Four Seasons</u>
	<u>North by Northwest</u>	<u>The Atlantic Monthly</u>
	<u>In the Shadow of a Rainbow: The True Story of a Friendship Between Man and Wolf</u>	<u>Frontline</u>

REMINDER▶ The titles of creative works such as books, movies, works of art, songs, articles, and poems are capitalized.

NOTE▶ The titles of poems, songs, short stories, essays, and articles are not underlined or italicized. These titles are set off in quotation marks.

EXAMPLES	"Mending Wall" [poem]
	"A Good Man Is Hard to Find" [short story]

EXERCISE A Underline any title that should be in italics in each of the following sentences. Be sure to underline every word of the title.

Examples 1. I have seen <u>It's a Wonderful Life</u> more than five times. [*It's a Wonderful Life* is underlined because it is the title of a movie.]

2. My sister tried out for a part in <u>Our Town</u>. [*Our Town* is underlined because it is the title of a play.]

1. Have you read <u>Treasure Island</u>? [What is the title of the book?]

2. <u>Dilbert</u> is my favorite comic strip. [What is the title of the comic strip?]

3. You have probably heard some of the music from Gershwin's long musical work <u>Rhapsody in Blue</u>.

4. Did you read the mummy article in the latest issue of <u>National Geographic</u>?

5. Leonard Bernstein's musical <u>West Side Story</u> is performed often.

Developmental Language Skills

115

6. The musical was based on a Shakespeare play, Romeo and Juliet.

7. Roll of Thunder, Hear My Cry is the title of a book on our reading list this year.

8. Many people recognize Water Lilies, a painting by Claude Monet.

9. I really enjoy watching old episodes of Star Trek: The Next Generation.

10. The illustrations in David Macaulay's book Pyramid are very detailed.

15b. Use underlining (italics) for the names of ships, trains, aircraft, and spacecraft.

The names of ships, trains, aircraft, and spacecraft are underlined or written in italics.

> **EXAMPLES** the Russian space station *Mir* [spacecraft]
> the *Titanic* [ship]
> the *Empire Builder* [train]
> the *Flyer* [airplane]

EXERCISE B Underline any words that should be set in italics in each of the following sentences.

Example 1. The Mayflower was the ship that brought the first Pilgrims to America. [*Mayflower* is underlined because it is the name of a ship.]

11. A train called the Sunset Limited runs all the way from Los Angeles to Florida. [What is the name of the train?]

12. Columbia was the name of the first U. S. space shuttle.

13. The plane that Lindbergh flew across the Atlantic Ocean was named the Spirit of St. Louis.

14. One of Columbus's three ships was called the Santa María.

15. Clipper ships like the Flying Cloud were designed to sail long distances.

EXERCISE C Complete each of the following sentences by writing a title in each blank. Be sure to underline each title.

Example 1. I'd like to learn more about the series of spacecraft called _____*Pathfinder*_____.

[*Pathfinder* is underlined because it is the name of a spacecraft.]

16. My favorite book is Dora's Wild Adventure. [What is the title of a book you like? Should it be underlined?]

17. The funniest movie I've ever seen is Disney's Snow White

18. A TV show I watched recently is called Barney.

19. NY Times is the name of a newspaper that tells about current events.

20. Titanicha is the name of a ship.

Quotation Marks A

15d. Use quotation marks to enclose a *direct quotation*—a person's exact words.

Be sure to place quotation marks both before and after a person's exact words.

EXAMPLES "Notice the lion's long, sharp teeth," said the narrator of the nature video. [Quotation marks surround the narrator's exact words, which begin the sentence.]

Lincoln began the Gettysburg Address with the words, "Four score and seven years ago." [Quotation marks surround Lincoln's exact words, which come at the end of the sentence.]

NOTE Exclamation points and question marks that are part of a direct quotation are placed inside the quotation marks. Also, a direct quotation usually begins with a capital letter.

EXERCISE A Place quotation marks wherever they are needed in each of the following sentences.

Example 1. "Please hand me your card," said the librarian. [The librarian said the exact words *Please hand me your card.* There are quotation marks at the beginning and the end of these words.]

1. Julie always says, It's better to be safe than sorry. [What are the exact words that Julie always says?]

2. Marty replied, I agree with everything that Diego just said.

3. Ohio is known as the Buckeye State, explained Martina.

4. What's the best way to get to Allentown Park? asked Chi.

5. A kidney bean is the same size as a newborn opossum, Mr. Webber informed us.

Sometimes, a person's exact words are interrupted by an explanation of who is talking. When this happens, just remember the rule: Put quotation marks before and after a person's exact words.

EXAMPLES "We need to be at the school by 3:00," the tour guide shouted, "so it's time to get back on the bus!" [Quotation marks surround all of the tour guide's exact words, even though the quotation is broken into two sections. The *s* in *so* is lowercase because the second part of the quotation isn't a complete sentence.]

"Whose sunglasses are these?" asked the principal. "This morning I found them in the cafeteria." [Quotation marks surround all of the principal's exact words, even though the quotation is broken into two sections. The *T* in *This* is capitalized because the second part of the quotation is a complete sentence.]

EXERCISE B Place quotation marks wherever they are needed in each of the following sentences.

Example 1. "Did you know," asked Ruben, "that the National Baseball Hall of Fame is in New York?" [Quotation marks surround all of Ruben's exact words.]

GO ON

6. I can't believe it, Jenna announced. I just won first prize at the county science fair! [Where are the two sections of Jenna's exact words?]

7. I may be about ten minutes late, said Gordon, because I have to run an errand before I meet up with you.

8. I'll need some time to think about it, Greg said. Ask me again tomorrow.

9. You are right, said Mrs. Cortez, that the only U.S. president to resign from office was Richard Nixon.

10. Before we paint the house, said the woman with the clipboard, another group of volunteers will scrape off the old paint first.

When you tell a story, you sometimes explain what somebody else said rather than repeat the person's exact words. When you reword what another person has said, you are using an indirect quotation.

Do not use quotation marks for an *indirect quotation*—a rewording of a direct quotation.

DIRECT QUOTATION	Steven asked, "When does the school year start?" [The quotation marks surround Steven's exact words.]
INDIRECT QUOTATION	Steven asked when the school year would start. [The sentence rewords what Steven said. Steven did not actually say, "When the school year would start," so no quotation marks surround these words.]

EXERCISE C Tell whether each of the following sentences has a direct quotation or an indirect quotation. On the line provided, write *D* for *direct quotation* or *I* for *indirect quotation*.

Example ___*I*___ **1.** Gwen said that science is her favorite class. [The sentence does not repeat Gwen's exact words. Gwen did not actually say the words, "that science is her favorite class," so no quotation marks surround these words.]

_____ **11.** "Please look into your microscopes," said Mrs. Cho. [Did Mrs. Cho actually say the words, "Please look into your microscopes"?]

_____ **12.** Gwen's lab partner asked Gwen how to adjust the focus.

_____ **13.** Gwen replied, "Use this knob to focus the microscope."

_____ **14.** "Those cells look huge!" exclaimed Gwen's lab partner.

_____ **15.** Gwen agreed and said that cells are much more interesting when you can actually see them.

Quotation Marks B

15j. When you write dialogue (a conversation), begin a new paragraph every time the speaker changes.

EXAMPLE "What are you doing after school today?" asked Maria.

"I'm not sure," said Camilla. "I promised to feed my neighbor's cat right after school, but I may have some free time after that. Why do you ask? Is there something that you want to do?" [Camilla says several sentences in a row. Quotation marks are not needed around every sentence, but only at the beginning and the end of her exact words.]

"Yes. I was wondering if you could help me with my history homework for a half hour or so after school." [Maria is speaking.]

"Sure, I'll help you." [Camilla is speaking.]

EXERCISE A Put a caret (^) in every place where a new paragraph should begin in the following sentences. Hint: A new paragraph should begin every time a different person talks.

Examples [1]^"Mom, are you going to the grocery store today?" asked Alice. [2]^"Yes," her mother answered. "I'm leaving for the store in a few minutes. Do you need anything?" [The first sentence needs to be indented because Alice is beginning the conversation. The second sentence needs to be indented because Alice's mom is a new speaker.]

[1] "Please bring me some pencils," asked Alice. "I also need notebook paper for school." [2] "Do you need those supplies for tonight's homework?" her mother asked. "I need to put gasoline in the car, too, so I probably won't be back until five o'clock." [3] "No, Mom," said Alice. "I have enough paper to finish my math problems." [4] "All right then, I'm heading out. If you need anything while I'm gone, just ask Dad." [5] "Okay, I will. I'll see you soon."

15l. Use single quotation marks to enclose a quotation within a quotation.

In some conversations, a person may ask about or repeat something that someone else has said. When you write down such a conversation, one quotation will be inside another. Use single quotation marks to surround the quotation that is on the inside.

EXAMPLE Jesse asked, "Did Dad say, 'Be home by ten o'clock'?" [Jesse's speech is directly quoted and is in double quotation marks. Jesse is also quoting something that Dad said. Dad's words are in single quotation marks. Since Jesse is the one who asked a question, the question mark is inside Jesse's double quotation marks only.]

GO ON

EXERCISE B Write *C* for *correct* on the line provided for each of the following sentences that correctly uses double and single quotation marks. Do not write anything next to the sentences that have quotation mark errors.

Example _____ **1.** Joe said, "I just heard Dora whisper, "Today is our teacher's birthday." "

[The punctuation is incorrect. Dora's exact words should be surrounded by single quotation marks.]

_____ **6.** Lori announced, "It's a snow day! I just heard the reporter say, 'All schools in Travis County are closed for the day.' " [Do double quotation marks surround everything Lori said? Do single quotation marks surround everything the reporter said?]

_____ **7.** "I was startled," said Jeb, "when I heard Sonia yell, The dishwasher is overflowing!"

_____ **8.** Mr. Ochoa told us, "I heard the principal say, "One of our teachers will win an award.' "

_____ **9.** The teacher told her class, "I thought someone just said, 'I have a question.' "

_____ **10.** Carl said, "I was surprised when I heard Nora say, 'I am a big fan of snakes and spiders.'

15m. | Use quotation marks to enclose the titles of short works such as short stories, poems, songs, episodes of television series, essays, articles, and chapters and other parts of books.

The titles of short stories, poems, songs, episodes of TV shows, articles, and chapters are enclosed in double quotation marks. Do not underline or use italics for these titles.

> **EXAMPLES** "Wildwood Flower" [song]
> "We Real Cool" [poem]
> "A Diamond as Big as the Ritz" [short story]
> "Bully on the Bus" [TV show episode]

EXERCISE C Place quotation marks wherever they are needed in the sentences below.

Example 1. Edgar Allan Poe wrote a poem called "Annabel Lee." [*Annabel Lee* is in quotation marks because it the title of a poem.]

11. Ms. Barnett's class will read a poem called The Raven for homework tonight. [What is the title of the poem?]

12. A silly version of Jingle Bells was playing on the radio.

13. Mr. Friedman loves the song It's a Wonderful World.

14. If our camping trip were made into a short story, a good name for it might be Surviving the Mosquitos.

15. I will base my poem on Stopping by Woods on a Snowy Evening by Robert Frost.

Apostrophes

Possessive Nouns

The possessive case of a noun is the form of the noun that shows ownership. This form is made by adding an apostrophe and often an s to the noun. Be careful where you place apostrophes, or you may confuse your reader.

15n. To form the possessive case of a singular noun, add an apostrophe and an s.

> **EXAMPLES** The **tiger's** teeth are very sharp. [The teeth belong to one tiger. The apostrophe comes after the singular noun *tiger* and before the s. The s in this example shows possession and does not make the noun *tiger* plural.]
>
> The **man's** shoes were bright green. [The shoes belong to one man. The apostrophe comes between *man* and the s that shows possession.]

15o. To form the possessive case of a plural noun that does not end in s, add an apostrophe and an s.

> **EXAMPLE** The **men's** shoes were wet and muddy. [The shoes belong to more than one man. The plural noun *men* does not end in s, so the apostrophe comes before the s.]

15p. To form the possessive case of a plural noun ending in s, add only the apostrophe.

> **EXAMPLE** The **tigers'** teeth are very sharp. [The teeth belong to more than one tiger. The noun *tigers* is the plural form of *tiger*, so the apostrophe follows the s.]

EXERCISE A Write the possessive form of each of the following words on the line provided.

Example 1. mice ___mice's___ [The word *mice* is plural and does not end in s. The possessive form is made by adding an apostrophe and and s.]

1. pictures _____ [Is the word *pictures* plural? Does it end in s?]

2. clown _____ [Is the word *clown* plural?]

3. store _____

4. children _____

5. dogs _____

6. girls _____

7. truck _____

8. umbrella _____

9. people _____

10. sisters _____

Possessive Pronouns

15q. Do not use an apostrophe with possessive personal pronouns.

> **EXAMPLE** Is this jacket **yours** or **hers**?

GO ON ▶

15r. To form the possessive case of some indefinite pronouns, add an apostrophe and an *s*.

> **EXAMPLE** Is this movie **everyone's** favorite movie? [The possessive form of *everyone* is formed by adding an *s* and an apostrophe.]

EXERCISE B Write the possessive form of each of the following words. Write your answer on the line provided.

Example 1. her ___*her*___ [*Her* is already possessive. It is not a word that forms its possessive by adding an apostrophe and an *s*.]

11. either _____ [Is *either* a word that forms its possessive by adding an apostrophe and an *s*?]

12. you _____

13. everybody _____

14. someone _____

15. him _____

Contractions

15s. Use an apostrophe to show where letters, words, or numerals have been omitted (left out) in a contraction.

A contraction is a shorter form of a word, a number, or a group of words. The apostrophe in a contraction shows where letters or numbers have been left out.

> **EXAMPLES** is + not = **isn't**   will + not = **won't**
> of + the + clock = **o'clock**   they + are = **they're**
> that + is = **that's**   1988 – 1900 = **'88**

NOTE Do not confuse contractions and possessive pronouns. Possessive personal pronouns do not have apostrophes.

> **EXAMPLES** It's too expensive. [*It's* is a contraction for *It is*.]

EXERCISE C Put apostrophes where they are needed in the following sentences.

Example 1. Don't you want to go to the movies? [*Don't* comes from *Do not*, so the apostrophe goes where the *o* has been left out of *not*.]

16. She hasnt forgotten my birthday. [Which letter has been left out of the words *has not*?]

17. Whats the name of his brother?

18. Youre in my math class this year.

19. Do you know whos making the posters for the play?

20. The banner in the gym congratulated the graduating class of 02.

Hyphens, Parentheses, Brackets, and Dashes

15v. Use a hyphen with compound numbers from twenty-one to ninety-nine.

Some words are always written with a hyphen. When you write out the numbers from twenty-one to ninety-nine, be sure to use a hyphen.

> **EXAMPLES** This poem has twenty-eight lines. [The number *twenty-eight* is written with a hyphen.]
>
> What will Claire do to celebrate the fact that she is turning eighty-two on Friday? [The age *eighty-two* is written with a hyphen.]

15w. Use a hyphen with the prefixes *ex–*, *self–*, *all–*, and *great–* and with the suffixes *–elect* and *–free*.

When most prefixes and suffixes are added to words, no hyphen is necessary between the word and the prefix or the suffix. Some prefixes and suffixes, such as the ones listed above, always need a hyphen.

> **EXAMPLES** great-grandfather [The prefix *great–* always needs a hyphen.]
>
> sugar-free [The suffix *–free* always needs a hyphen.]
>
> fishing [The suffix *–ing* does not need a hyphen.]
>
> unnecessary [The prefix *un–* does not need a hyphen.]

EXERCISE A Insert hyphens where they are needed in the following phrases.

Example 1. the president elect of our club [The suffix *–elect* always needs a hyphen. The word *president-elect* needs a hyphen.]

1. an all purpose device [Does the prefix *all–* always need a hyphen?]

2. the ex mayor of the city

3. seventy six trombones

4. my great grandmother

5. only ninety five cents

15x. Use parentheses to enclose material that is added to a sentence but is not considered of major importance.

Parentheses are used to tell the reader that the information enclosed is not important but might be interesting or useful to know. Do not enclose important information in parentheses.

> **EXAMPLE** Beethoven (1770–1827) was a German composer. [The dates in parentheses tell when Beethoven was born and when he died. These dates are in parentheses because they are not important to the point of the sentence. Instead, they add helpful, but not necessary, information. This is a very common use of parentheses.]

GO ON

Developmental Language Skills

15y.   Use brackets to enclose an explanation added to quoted or parenthetical material.

Brackets are used to add an explanation inside material in quotation marks or in material that is already inside parentheses.

EXAMPLES   The witness said, "I saw him [Mr. Smith] at the store before the robbery." [The information in brackets tells the reader who *him* is. The witness did not speak the words *Mr. Smith*. The writer added the information.]

For more information on polar bears, turn to the chart at the end of this chapter. (See page 21 for a chart [Figure 1] with more facts on polar bears.) [*Figure 1* is in brackets because it has been added as a side note to information that is already in parentheses.]

15z.   Use a dash to indicate an abrupt break in thought or speech.

Dashes, like parentheses, are used to set off extra information. Dashes are usually considered stronger or more forceful than parentheses. When you want the reader to notice the additional information, use dashes instead of parentheses.

EXAMPLE   This is the best—I mean the very best—picture I've ever drawn! [The writer interrupts the sentence to add additional information. The writer wants the reader to notice the additional information.]

EXERCISE B   The following sentences need parentheses, dashes, or brackets. Correct each sentence by inserting the punctuation mark named in front of each item number.

Example   *brackets*   **1.** The coach said, "I'm happy to accept this award [the sportsmanship trophy] on behalf of the school." [The writer added the words *the sportsmanship trophy* to the coach's quotation, so brackets need to be around these words.]

dashes   **6.** Did you see that there it goes again huge owl? [Which words interrupt the sentence?]

parentheses   **7.** Mark Twain (his real name was Samuel Clemens 1835–1910) created the characters Tom Sawyer and Huckleberry Finn. [Which dates have been added as a side note to information that is already in parentheses?]

brackets   **8.** An eyewitness said, "It the blue truck ran a red light."

dashes   **9.** Elena's mother she was born in Costa Rica is a newspaper photographer.

parentheses   **10.** Abraham Lincoln 1809–1865 was the sixteenth president of the United States.

parentheses   **11.** Jarrod's sister second from the left in the picture lives in San Diego.

dashes   **12.** Underneath the porch was I'm not kidding the biggest rattlesnake I've ever seen!

parentheses   **13.** The movie was short less than one hour but seemed longer.

dashes   **14.** The next story we'll be reading is please settle down by a well-known local writer.

parentheses   **15.** Use a pen black or blue ink only to complete the application.

Words with *ie* and *ei*

16a. Write *ie* when the sound is long *e*, except after *c*.

The long *e* sound is what you hear in words such as *relief, sleep,* and *peace.*

Write *ei* when the sound is not long *e*, especially when the sound is long *a*.

EXAMPLES	*i* before *e:*	*ei* after *c:*	*ei* pronounced *ay:*
	belief	ceiling	neighbor
	field	conceit	freight
	niece	deceit	weigh
	shield	perceive	vein
	chief	receive	sleigh
	yield		
	piece		
	achieve		

TIP▶ If you are having trouble with the above guidelines, it is always good to remember the old rhyme: **i** *before* **e,** *except after* **c** *(or when pronounced* **ay,** *as in neighbor and weigh.)*

EXERCISE A Circle the word in parentheses that is spelled correctly in each of the following sentences.

Examples 1. The kitten is always getting into (mischief) mischeif). [The letters do not immediately

follow *c*, and the letters are not pronounced *ay*. The correct spelling is *mischief.*]

2. The miners were searching for a (vien, (vein)) of gold deep inside the earth. [The

letters are pronounced *ay*. The correct spelling is *vein*.]

1. The (*fierce, feirce*) roar of the lion carried across the plains. [Do the letters follow *c*? Are they

pronounced *ay*?]

2. At summer camp, we began our swimming lessons sitting in a group on the (*pier, peir*). [Do

the letters follow *c*? Are they pronounced *ay*?]

3. The teacher drew a circle on the board and divided it into (*ieght, eight*) sections.

4. Each one of the (*pieces, peices*) represented a fraction of the whole circle.

5. Willie, my (*nieghbor, neighbor*), raises beagles.

6. At each visit, the nurse records my (*wieght, weight*) on a growth chart.

7. The parrot (*shrieked, shreiked*) when the dog barked.

8. Have the Franklins opened (*thier, their*) new restaurant yet?

9. Felicia's latest painting was on the (*cieling, ceiling*)!

10. Marco gave his mother a wad of crumpled bills and (*reciepts, receipts*).

Developmental Language Skills

GO ON ▶

> **TIP** Because there are so many exceptions to spelling rules, it is always a good idea to use a dictionary if you are not sure how to spell a word.

EXERCISE B Circle the word in parentheses that is spelled correctly in each of the following sentences.

Examples 1. During the (*interview*, *interveiw*), I was asked many questions. [The letters do not immediately follow *c*, and the letters are not pronounced *ay*. The correct spelling is *interview*.]

2. My latest film was well (*recieved*, *received*) at the box office. [The letters immediately follow *c*. The correct spelling is *received*.]

11. I work in an unusual (*field*, *feild*). [Do the letters follow *c*? Are they pronounced *ay*?]

12. I am a stuntwoman for the movies: I change places with the star just before she bails out of an airplane or leaps from a (*frieght*, *freight*) train. [Do the letters follow *c*? Are they pronounced *ay*?]

13. The public never (*percieves*, *perceives*) the switch.

14. Have you ever been (*decieved*, *deceived*) by someone like me?

15. Soon, however, I will be flying home to visit my (*nieces*, *neices*) and nephews.

16. It has been (*ieght*, *eight*) months since I have been home.

17. This trip will be too (*brief*, *breif*).

18. It will be a (*relief*, *releif*) to take a break from my busy schedule.

19. Perhaps an early snowstorm will (*yield*, *yeild*) enough snow for sledding!

20. Even if it doesn't snow, my (*chief*, *cheif*) goal will be relaxation.

Prefixes and Suffixes

Prefixes

A *prefix* is a group of letters added to the beginning of a word to change its meaning. When adding a prefix to a word, do not change the spelling of the word itself.

    EXAMPLES   un + happy = un**happy**   il + legal = il**legal**   in + direct = in**direct**

EXERCISE A   Add the prefix to the word for each of the following items. Write the new word on the line provided.

Example 1. over + load = ___overload___ [Adding the prefix *over* does not change the spelling of

        the word *load*.]

1. in + expensive = _____ [Will   **4.** un + kind = _____

adding the prefix *in* change the spelling of the   **5.** dis + prove = _____

word *expensive*?]   **6.** re + organize = _____

2. dis + qualify = _____ [Will   **7.** in + operative = _____

adding the prefix *dis* change the spelling of the   **8.** il + logical = _____

word *qualify*?]   **9.** im + balance = _____

3. im + patient = _____   **10.** dis + honest = _____

Suffixes

A *suffix* is a letter or a group of letters added to the end of a word to change its meaning.

16e.   Drop the final silent *e* before adding a suffix beginning with a vowel.

A silent *e* is not pronounced when you say the word.

    EXAMPLES   write + ing = **writ**ing   like + able = **lik**able

TIP ▶ *Vowels* are the letters *a, e, i, o, u,* and sometimes *y. Consonants* are all the other letters.

16f.   Keep the final silent *e* before adding a suffix that begins with a consonant.

    EXAMPLES   care + less = **care**less   place + ment = **place**ment

EXERCISE B   Add the suffix to the word for each of the following items. Write the new word on the line provided.

Examples 1. care + ing = ___caring___ [The suffix begins with the vowel *i*, so the final silent *e* is

        dropped.]

     2. waste + ful = ___wasteful___ [The suffix begins with the consonant *f*, so the final silent

        e is kept.]

GO ON ▶

11. love + ing = _____ [Does the

suffix begin with a vowel or a consonant?]

12. retire + ment = _____ [Does the

suffix begin with a vowel or a consonant?]

13. suspense + ful = _____

14. convince + ing = _____

15. spice + y = _____

16. become + ing = _____

17. decorate + ed = _____

18. skate + ing = _____

19. advertise + ment = _____

20. hope + ful = _____

16h. Double the final consonant before adding –ing,–ed,–er, or –est to a one-syllable word if the word ends in a single consonant preceded by a single vowel.

Look at the word *chop*. It has one syllable. The final consonant (*p*) is preceded by a vowel (*o*). If we add –ing, we double the *p*: cho**pp**ing.

    EXAMPLES hit + ing = hi**tt**ing   top + ing = to**pp**ing

                  stop + ed = sto**pp**ed   mop + ed = mo**pp**ed

Do not double the final consonant in words ending in *w* or *x*.

    EXAMPLES plow + ing = plo**w**ing   tax + ing = ta**x**ing

Do not double the consonant before adding –ing, –ed, –er, or –est to a one-syllable word if the word ends in a single consonant that is preceded by more than one vowel. Do not double the consonant before adding –ing, –ed, –er, or –est to most words of more than one syllable.

    EXAMPLES leap + ing = lea**p**ing   explain + ed = explai**n**ed

NOTE▶ Whenever you are not sure how to spell a word with a suffix, look the word up in a dictionary.

EXERCISE C Circle the correct spelling of the word in parentheses in each of the following sentences.

Example 1. We are (⟨mapping⟩, maping) the best route to the ballpark. [The one-syllable word *map* ends in a single consonant, so the final consonant, *p*, is doubled.]

21. Farmer Murphy's old tractor sat (*rustting, rusting*) in the field. [Does the one-syllable word *rust* end with a consonant preceded by a vowel?]

22. The (*swimers, swimmers*) raced to the other end of the pool.

23. The big dog (*skidded, skided*) on the ice.

24. Of all of us, Bianca keeps her locker the (*neattest, neatest*).

25. Jon had to have his old truck (*towwed, towed*) to the repair shop.

Plurals of Nouns

Most nouns can be made plural simply by adding –*s* to the end of the word.

SINGULAR	joke	carrot	holiday	radio
PLURAL	joke**s**	carrot**s**	holiday**s**	radio**s**

Some nouns are made plural by adding –*es* to the end of the word.

SINGULAR	glass	flash	potato	Gomez
PLURAL	glass**es**	flash**es**	potato**es**	Gomez**es**

TIP Say the words quietly to yourself. If the plural word has one more syllable than the singular word has, the plural word is probably spelled with –*es*. A syllable is a word part that can be pronounced as one uninterrupted sound.

   EXAMPLE   The singular word glass has one syllable. The plural word glasses has two
   syllables: *glass • es.* The plural word *glasses* is formed by adding –*es* to the
   singular word *glass.*

EXERCISE A Write the plural form of each of the following words. Use the line that is provided after each word.

Examples 1. freeway ___*freeways*___ [The plural *freeways* has the same number of syllables as the singular freeway. The plural is formed by adding –*s*.]

   2. catch ___*catches*___ [The plural *catches* has one more syllable than the singular catch. The plural is formed by adding –*es*.]

1. flag _____ [Does the plural form have the same number of syllables as the singular or does the plural form have one more syllable?]

2. cave _____ [Does the plural form have the same number of syllables as the singular or does the plural form have one more syllable?]

3. itch _____

4. telescope _____

5. toss _____

6. crutch _____

7. photograph _____

8. box _____

9. actress _____

10. bicycle _____

GO ON →

The plurals of some nouns are formed in different ways. Many words that end in —*y* form the plural by changing the *y* to *i* before adding —*es*.

SINGULAR fly   pony   strawberry

PLURAL fl**ies**   pon**ies**   strawberr**ies**

Some nouns change in other ways to form the plural. A few nouns do not change at all to form the plural.

SINGULAR man   shelf   deer

PLURAL men   shelves   deer

REMINDER If you are not sure how to spell the plural of a word, look the word up in the dictionary. Keep in mind that many dictionaries will only show the plural form of a word if the plural is not formed simply by adding —*s*.

EXERCISE B Write the plural form of each of the following words. Use the line that is provided after each word.

Examples 1. life   ___*lives*___   [The *f* in *life* changes to a *v* and an *s* is added to form the plural.]

2. mouse ___*mice*___   [The singular *mouse* changes to *mice* to form the plural.]

11. self   _____   [Do any letters in *self* change before —*es* is added to form the plural?]

12. tooth   _____   [Do any letters in *tooth* change to form the plural?]

13. child   _____

14. leaf   _____

15. goose   _____

16. woman _____

17. trout   _____

18. calf   _____

19. foot   _____

20. sheep   _____

Words Often Confused A

People often confuse the following words. Some of these words are *homonyms*—that is, their pronunciations are the same. However, these words have different meanings and spellings. Other words in the following groups have the same or similar spellings yet have different meanings.

already [adverb] *previously; something accomplished by or before the specified time*
Karla has **already** finished her homework.

all ready [adjective] *all prepared; in readiness*
The musicians are **all ready** to begin.

altogether [adverb] *entirely; everything included; everything being considered*
There are **altogether** too many people at this table.

all together [adjective] *in the same place*
They are **all together** in the kitchen.

[adverb] *at the same time*
All together, the band began to play.

EXERCISE A Circle the word or words in parentheses that will complete the sentence correctly.

Examples 1. The athletes were (all ready, already) to start the race. [The meaning is *all prepared; in readiness.*]

2. Students from around the state were (altogether, all together) at the conference. [The meaning is *in the same place.*]

1. It was (*already, all ready*) time to board the plane. [Is the meaning *previously; something accomplished by or before the specified time* or *all prepared; in readiness?*]

2. The crowd was (*altogether, all together*) too noisy for me. [Is the meaning *entirely; everything included; everything being considered* or *in the same place* or *at the same time?*]

3. The events for the charity drive were (*altogether, all together*) a success.

4. Finishing the song (*all together, altogether*) was the choir's goal for this rehearsal.

5. We were (*already, all ready*), but the bus was late.

6. The field was (*altogether, all together*) too muddy to play the game.

7. By the time we arrived, Joe had (*all ready, already*) run his race.

8. The audience was (*already, all ready*) for the play to begin.

9. The actors were (*all ready, already*) as the curtain rose.

10. We were told to stay (*all together, altogether*) during the tour.

> **brake** [noun] *a device to stop a machine*
> Always use the emergency **brake** when parking on a hill.
>
> **break** [verb] *to fracture; to shatter*
> Even if you drop this plastic bottle, it won't **break.**
>
> **choose** [verb, rhymes with *shoes*] *to select*
> Today, it is Robin's turn to **choose** a partner.
>
> **chose** [verb, past tense of *choose*; rhymes with *rose*]
> Phillip **chose** his partner yesterday.
>
> **cloths** [noun] *pieces of cloth*
> The painter used drop **cloths** to protect the floors.
>
> **clothes** [noun] *wearing apparel; clothing*
> We gave my grandmother new **clothes** for her birthday.

EXERCISE B Circle the word or words in parentheses that will complete the sentence correctly.

Examples 1. Tomorrow we will buy new school (cloths, (clothes). [The meaning is *wearing apparel; clothing.*]

2. It is difficult to (choose, chose) from among all the flavors. [The meaning is *to select.*]

11. The bicycle (*break, brake*) must be replaced. [Is the meaning *a device to stop a machine* or *to fracture; to shatter?*]

12. We will need some soft (*clothes, cloths*) to clean the car. [Is the meaning *pieces of cloth* or *wearing apparel; clothing?*]

13. Yesterday, the students (*chose, choose*) their candidates for the class president.

14. Please don't (*break, brake*) that vase.

15. Sometimes, it is difficult to (*chose, choose*) the right thing to do.

16. I will wear new (*clothes, cloths*) to my birthday party.

17. Did she (*break, brake*) the school record?

18. Mr. Sanchez set the parking (*brake, break*) before he got out of the car.

19. Kathleen (*choose, chose*) a dark green backpack.

20. My father has some old drop (*clothes, cloths*) rolled up in the shed.

Words Often Confused B

People often confuse the following words. Some of these words are *homonyms*—that is, their pronunciations are the same. However, these words have different meanings and spellings. Other words in the following groups have the same or similar spellings yet have different meanings.

coarse [adjective] *rough; crude; not fine*
The bread was sprinkled with **coarse** salt.

course [noun] *path of action; series of studies;* [also used in the expression *of course*]
The sailors mapped the best **course** to sail.
Of **course** you may read your poem.

desert [noun, pronounced *des' • ert*] *a dry, barren, sandy region; a wilderness*
Riding their camels, the nomads wandered across the **desert.**

desert [verb, pronounced *de • sert'*] *to abandon; to leave*
A good sportsman would never **desert** his team.

dessert [noun, pronounced *des • sert'*] *a sweet, final course of a meal*
My favorite **dessert** is frozen grapes.

TIP A way to remember how to spell *dessert* is to pretend that the extra *s* stands for *sweet*.

hear [verb] *to receive sounds through the ears*
Every night I **hear** dogs barking in the distance.

here [adverb] *in this place*
I live in Texas now, but I grew up **here.**

EXERCISE A Circle the word or words in parentheses that will complete the sentence correctly.

Examples 1. The carpenter used (*coarse*, *course*) sandpaper. [The meaning is *rough; crude; not fine.*]

2. The weather in the (*dessert*, *desert*) is hot and dry. [The meaning is a *dry, barren, sandy region; a wilderness.*]

1. Was the (*desert*, *dessert*) last night made with apples? [Is the meaning *a dry, barren, sandy region; a wilderness* or *a sweet, final course of a meal*?]

2. I will be (*here*, *hear*) for an hour. [Is the meaning *to receive sounds through the ears* or *in this place*?]

3. The beach was covered with (*coarse*, *course*) sand.

4. My father is taking a night (*course*, *coarse*) in computer graphics.

5. Carry extra water when driving through the (*dessert*, *desert*).

6. Can you (*hear*, *here*) the band practicing at the high school?

7. After the spaghetti dinner, I had no room for (*desert*, *dessert*).

GO ON

Developmental Language Skills

8. Dogs can (*here, hear*) very high-pitched sounds.

9. The Bedouins, who live in the (*desert, dessert*), use camels for transportation.

10. The soldiers were forced to (*dessert, desert*) the broken-down jeep.

---

lead	[verb, rhymes with *feed*] *to go first; to guide or direct* The drum major will **lead** the parade.
led	[verb, past tense of *lead*] *went first* Dr. Martin Luther King, Jr., **led** the civil rights movement.
lead	[noun, rhymes with *red*] *a heavy metal; graphite used in a pencil* People who take X-rays wear **lead** aprons for protection.
loose	[adjective, rhymes with *goose*] *not tight; free; not confined* The screws on the cabinet were too **loose.**
lose	[verb, rhymes with *snooze*] *to suffer loss* I will try not to **lose** my new glasses.

EXERCISE B Circle the word or words in parentheses that will complete the sentence correctly.

Examples 1. The tour guide will (**lead**, *led*) you through the historic house. [The meaning is *to go first; to guide or direct.*]

2. How did the dog get (*lose,* **loose**)? [The meaning is *not tight; free; not confined.*]

11. (*Lead, Led*) is often used to make batteries. [Is the meaning *went first* or *a heavy metal; graphite used in a pencil*?]

12. Katie's mittens were clipped to her jacket so that she would not (*loose, lose*) them. [Is the meaning *not tight; free; not confined* or *to suffer loss*?]

13. The host country will (*led, lead*) the parade of flags.

14. A good sport knows how to (*loose, lose*) graciously.

15. The woman who formerly (*led, lead*) the company has retired.

16. Oh, no! Who let the goose (*lose, loose*)?

17. Our teacher warned us, "If you snooze, you (*loose, lose*)."

18. The latch on the door was (*lose, loose*), and the puppy got out.

19. The horses had to be (*led, lead*) out of the burning barn.

20. Did you break the (*led, lead*) in your pencil again?

Words Often Confused C

People often confuse the following words. Some of these words are *homonyms*—that is, their pronunciations are the same. However, these words have different meanings and spellings. Other words in the following groups have the same or similar spellings yet have different meanings.

passed [verb, past tense of pass] *went by; successfully completing a course of study*
The parade slowly **passed** by the crowd.
I **passed** my math test.

past [noun] *time that has gone by; a previous time*
In the **past,** people walked more than they do today.

[preposition] *beyond*
The band has marched **past** the viewing stand.

[adjective] *ended; gone by; elapsed in time*
During the **past** year, I have skated only once.

peace [noun] *quiet order and security; stillness; absence of struggle or war*
Many nations strive for world **peace.**

piece [noun] *a part of something*
No one wanted to take the last **piece** of cornbread.

TIP▶ Here is a way to remember the difference between *peace* and *piece*. You eat a **pie**ce of **pie**.

EXERCISE A Circle the word or words in parentheses that will complete the sentence correctly.

Example 1. In the (*past*, *passed*) week, I have walked to school twice. [The meaning is *ended; gone by; elapsed in time.*]

1. What can an individual do to promote international (*piece*, *peace*)? [Is the meaning *absence of struggle or war* or *a part of something*?]

2. In the (*passed*, *past*), space ships were only fiction.

3. May I please have another (*peace*, *piece*) of turkey?

4. The tea cup fell and broke into several (*peaces*, *pieces*).

5. The Canadian runner was in the lead when the Nigerian (*past*, *passed*) her.

GO ON ▶

principal [noun] *the head of a school*
Our **principal** came to the assembly.

[adjective] *chief; main; most important*
He spoke about his **principal** duties.

principle [noun] *a rule of conduct; a fundamental truth*
Our principal is an honest man guided by his **principles.**

to [preposition] *in the direction of; toward*
[also used before the root form of a verb, such as *to be* or *to have*]
He went **to** the store **to** buy groceries.
She wants **to** be a doctor someday.

too [adverb] *also, more than enough*
Leanne wants to go, **too.**
I think I have cut **too** many pieces.

two [adjective or noun] *one plus one*
Josie could only find one of her **two** books.

EXERCISE B Circle the word or words in parentheses that will complete the sentence correctly.

Examples 1. Mr. Pellotta has been the school (*principle* (*principal*)) for many years. [The meaning is *the head of a school.*]

2. Lance will be taking the course, ((*too*), *to*, *two*). [The meaning is *also, more than enough.*]

6. That one is a robin, (*to*, *too*, *two*). [Is the meaning *in the direction of, also,* or *one plus one*?]

7. The (*principal*, *principle*) idea was stated in the first paragraph. [Is the meaning *chief; main; most important* or *a rule of conduct; a fundamental truth*?]

8. Is the mixture a ratio of eight (*two*, *too*, *to*) five?

9. I hope (*two*, *to*) attend Stanford University.

10. Myra went to her violin lesson at (*to*, *too*, *two*) o'clock.

11. Playing the violin was not (*too*, *to*, *two*) difficult for Marie.

12. Dr. Martin Luther King, Jr., was a man of (*principle*, *principal*).

13. Has Marco already gone (*to*, *too*, *two*) the park?

14. (*To*, *Too*, *Two*) of the trees still have their leaves.

15. Either your teacher or the (*principal*, *principle*) will answer your question.

Common Errors Review

Common Usage Errors

Be sure that you proofread each writing assignment before you turn it in. Errors in your writing can confuse and distract your readers. In fact, readers may form a poor impression of a writer who makes careless errors. Look for errors, especially in the following areas:

Do subjects and verbs agree?   Are modifiers in the correct form?
Do pronouns and antecedents agree?   Are modifiers placed correctly?
Are verb forms and tenses correct?   Is usage appropriate for audience and purpose?

After you make corrections or changes, read your writing again. Sometimes a change you make will create a new problem in another part of your writing.

The two following exercises will help you recognize and correct common errors in usage and mechanics.

EXERCISE A The following paragraph contains common errors in usage. Review the list of problem areas above and correct the errors. Use proofreading marks to make your corrections.

Examples 1. When the storm began, my brother and I was still at school. [The past tense of the

verb *begin* is *began*. The singular verb *was* should be the plural *were* because the

compound subject, *my brother and I*, is plural.]

2. The sky grew darkly, and than the rain poured down. [The verb *grew* is a linking

verb and should be followed by the adjective *dark*, not the adverb *darkly*. The adverb

then means "next" or "after that." The conjunction *than* is used in comparisons, and is

incorrect here.]

1. Water filled the parking lots quick, and streams are running across the streets.

2. Lightning ripped through the clouds, and the most loud thunder that I has ever heard
rumbled and boomed.

3. Soon the lights gone out, and all the students came out of his or her classrooms.

4. Laughing and joking, the halls were filled with alot of students.

5. Some classes went to the gym with there teachers, and others set in the cafeteria.

6. We couldn't hardly see our hands in front of our faces, accept when the lightning flashed.

7. One student wanted to call their parents, but the phones wasn't working.

8. After an hour, the electricity came back on sudden, and sunshine breaked through the clouds.

9. When we looked outside, we seen huge branches laying on the ground all around the school.

10. Everyone are still talking about the storm and all the damage they caused.

Developmental Language Skills

Common Mechanics Errors

When you write, always check your capitalization, punctuation, and spelling. Use a dictionary if you are not sure of a spelling or a word division. Make sure you haven't confused two words that sound alike but are spelled differently. These details make a big difference in your writing! Look for errors in the following areas, too:

Does every sentence begin with a capital letter?
Are all proper nouns capitalized?
Does every sentence end with an appropriate end mark?
Have you placed commas where they are needed?
Are direct quotations and titles capitalized and punctuated correctly?
Are words spelled and divided correctly?

EXERCISE B The following paragraph contains errors in mechanics. Correct the errors in capitalization, punctuation, and spelling. Use proofreading marks to make your corrections.

Examples 1. Have you ever visited the grayson county history museum. [*Grayson County History Museum* should be capitalized because it is the name of a particular building. The sentence should end with a question mark because it asks a question.]

2. Before my social studies class went there on a field trip I didn't know anything about local History. [A comma should follow *trip* to separate the introductory clause from the main sentence. The contraction *didn't* should have an apostrophe to show where letters have been left out. The word *history* is used here as a common noun and should not be capitalized.]

11. The museum is run by volunteers from the grayson county historical society

12. When you enter the building youll see a huge painting called The Past and the Future.

13. did you know that People have lived in this area for thousands of years

14. Display cases are filled with interesting objects and old photographs hang on the walls.

15. Our guide mr simpson pointed to one photograph and said My great grandfather built that bridge across the freeman river.

16. The picture showed horse drawn wagons crossing the bridge it must have been taken many years ago.

17. The people look hot and uncomfortable in they're heavy dark cloths.

18. If you want my advise you should visit the museum

19. Its open every thursday friday and saturday (accept for christmas and other holidays).

20. The museum is free but a sign near the door says please make a donation to help the museum.

Complete Sentences and Sentence Fragments

Complete Sentences

A *sentence* is a word group that contains a subject and a verb and that expresses a complete thought. Notice that sentences begin with a capital letter and end with a period, a question mark, or an exclamation point.

EXAMPLES	**T**yrone went to the store**.** [The subject is *Tyrone.* The verb is *went.* The word group expresses a complete thought and is, therefore, a sentence.]
	Didn't Tyrone go to the store**?** [The subject is *Tyrone.* The verb is *Did go.* The word group expresses a complete thought and is, therefore, a sentence.]
	Go to the store**.** [The subject *you* is understood. The verb is *Go.* The word group expresses a complete thought and is, therefore, a sentence.]
	What an easy chore that was**!** [The subject is *that.* The verb is *was.* The word group expresses a complete thought and is, therefore, a sentence.]

EXERCISE A Use proofreading marks to add capital letters and appropriate end marks to the following word groups to make them sentences.

Example 1. what a delicious smell that is**!** [Capitalize the first letter of the first word of a sentence. This sentence should end with an exclamation point.]

1. don't forget the list [Is the first word correctly capitalized? Is an appropriate end mark used?]

2. mom and Aunt Rosa need a loaf of bread

3. did you count your change

4. look out for traffic

5. was the dinner as great as it smelled

Sentence Fragments

Incomplete sentences are called sentence fragments. A *sentence fragment* is a word or word group that looks like a sentence but that does not have a subject, does not have a verb, or does not express a complete thought. Because it is incomplete, a sentence fragment can confuse your reader.

FRAGMENT	Was in the middle of the yard. [The word group does not have a subject. What was in the middle of the yard?]
SENTENCE	**The dog** was in the middle of the yard. [*The dog* was added to make a complete sentence.]
FRAGMENT	One of the best schools Francine's School of Music. [The word group does not have a verb. What about Francine's School of Music?]
SENTENCE	One of the best schools **is** Francine's School of Music. [The verb *is* is added to make a complete sentence.]

> **FRAGMENT** After you left. [The fragment does not express a complete thought. What happened after you left?]
>
> **SENTENCE** **Jane called** after you left. [The subject *Jane* and the verb *called* were added to make a complete sentence.]

EXERCISE B Identify each of the following word groups as a sentence fragment or a complete sentence. On the line provided, write *F* for each sentence fragment. Write *S* for each sentence.

Example __F__ **1.** The pink color of the flamingoes. [This word group does not have a verb and does not express a complete thought.]

_____ **6.** During the first few minutes of the performance. [Does the word group have both a subject and a verb? Does it express a complete thought?]

_____ **7.** What is your point?

_____ **8.** Which were often decorated with the club's mark.

_____ **9.** Explorer who risked his life in the Antarctic.

_____ **10.** What a beautiful sunset this is!

EXERCISE C Rewrite each sentence fragment, adding words to make the fragment a complete sentence. If an item is already a sentence, write *S* on the line provided.

Example 1. Were following close behind the mother duck. [Who or what was following? The word group does not have a subject.] *Six ducklings were following close behind the mother duck.*

11. Just across the border Canada's vast mountain range. [Is the word group missing a subject or a verb? Does it express a complete thought?] _____

_____

12. How funny that video was! _____

13. Gave everyone a copy of the announcement. _____

14. When she visited her grandparents. _____

_____

15. Mexican silver jewelry hanging behind the counter? _____

_____

Run-on Sentences

Identifying Run-on Sentences

A *run-on sentence* is a word group that is made up of two complete sentences that have been run together. The sentences either have no punctuation between them or have only a comma between them. Run-on sentences make it hard for the reader to tell where one thought ends and another begins.

RUN-ON	Give Jane a call she would like to talk to you. [No punctuation separates the two complete sentences.]
CORRECT	Give Jane a call. She would like to talk to you. [A period separates the two sentences.]
RUN-ON	The ball bounced away, a neighbor threw it back. [Only a comma separates the two complete sentences.]
CORRECT	The ball bounced away, **but** a neighbor threw it back. [A comma and the conjunction *but* separate the two sentences.]

EXERCISE A Decide which of the following word groups are run-on sentences. If a word group is a run-on, write *run-on* on the line provided. If the word group is correct, write *C* on the line provided.

Example _*run-on*_ **1.** Jesse plays drums Lee plays guitar. [This word group has two complete sentences, but there is no punctuation between them.]

_____ **1.** The Roman Empire fell centuries ago Roman structures still stand. [Does the correct punctuation separate the complete sentences?]

_____ **2.** The riverboat moved slowly, we made good time.

_____ **3.** There has been very little rainfall this summer, wildlife is coming closer to the city in search of water.

_____ **4.** Felicia adjusted the microscope. She still couldn't see any bacteria.

_____ **5.** Uncle Pedro is our favorite visitor, he always brings his guitar and a song.

Correcting Run-on Sentences

Here are two ways you can correct run-on sentences.

1. Make two sentences.

RUN-ON	The ball bounced away, a neighbor threw it back.
CORRECT	The ball bounced away. A neighbor threw it back.

2. Insert a comma and a coordinating conjunction such as *and, but,* or *or.*

RUN-ON	The ball bounced away a neighbor threw it back.
CORRECT	The ball bounced away, **but** a neighbor threw it back.

EXERCISE B Rewrite each run-on sentence by making two sentences or by inserting a comma and a conjunction to separate the two sentences that have been run together. If a sentence is not a run-on, write *Correct* on the line provided.

Examples 1. Don't worry, the coat can be washed. [Only a comma separates the two complete

sentences. The run-on needs to be revised.] *Don't worry. The coat can be washed.*

_____

2. Jim's dragon was made of green velvet, and it had red, glass eyes. [A comma and

the conjunction *and* separate the two complete sentences.] *Correct*_____

_____

6. We brought logs in from outside, soon a fire blazed in the fireplace. [Is the sentence correctly

punctuated? Do a conjunction and a comma separate the two complete sentences?] _____

_____

7. You really should try this salsa, it's made of onions, peppers, and lots of fresh tomatoes. [Is the

sentence correctly punctuated?] _____

_____

8. A green wall might be nice in your room or you could hang a poster. _____

_____

9. The moon was full, and we could see clearly that night. _____

_____

10. Some residents of the small town put up tall fences the deer just jump over them. _____

_____

11. A truck had recently painted lines on the road, orange cones blocked traffic. _____

_____

12. Dad got the oil pan and oilcans out, but he has not changed the oil yet. _____

_____

13. A mass of electrical wire snaked behind the desk, three computers shared the same table. _____

_____

14. The white cottages had been built ninety years ago, they have endured six hurricanes. _____

_____

15. I am walking the dog, will you come with me? _____

_____

Combining Sentences by Inserting Words and Phrases

Inserting Words

One way to combine short sentences is to take an important word from one sentence and insert it into another sentence. Sometimes you will have to change the form of the word before you insert it. You can change some words by adding an ending such as *–ed*, *–ing*, *–ful*, or *–ly*. Other words can be used without changing form.

ORIGINAL SENTENCES   The teacher gave us back our reports. She is very kind.

COMBINED SENTENCE   The teacher **kindly** gave us back our reports. [The two original sentences are combined by adding *kindly* to the first sentence.]

EXERCISE A   Use proofreading marks to combine each of the following pairs of sentences. Take the underlined word from one sentence and insert it into the other sentence. Be sure to make any necessary changes that are indicated in parentheses.

Example 1. My parents are ^*eagerly* awaiting the arrival of my grandmother. ~~They are eager~~. (Add *–ly*.)

[The two sentences are combined by adding *eagerly* to the first sentence.]

1. A weekend at our house usually involves cleaning and cooking. That's a <u>typical</u> weekend.

[Where should the underlined word be placed in the first sentence?]

2. The placement of the paintings was <u>strange</u>. The paintings were placed on the wall. (Add *–ly*.)

3. We would like to <u>rest</u> on vacation. We hope this will be a pleasant vacation. (Add *–ful*.)

4. Has the bell rung yet? It's the <u>last</u> bell.

5. The children at Claire's birthday party had a lot of fun. There were <u>thirteen</u> children.

Inserting Phrases

Another way to combine sentences is to take a phrase from one sentence and insert it into another sentence. A *phrase* is a group of related words that acts as a single part of speech. A phrase does not have both a subject and a verb.

ORIGINAL SENTENCES   Rosie is a new student. She is in my class.

COMBINED SENTENCE   Rosie is a new student **in my class.** [The phrase *in my class* is taken from the second sentence and inserted into the first.]

ORIGINAL SENTENCES   Tim's family will make sure that they have enough food for the trip. Tim's family will go to the supermarket.

COMBINED SENTENCE   **To make sure that they have enough food for the trip,** Tim's family will go to the supermarket. [*To* is added to the verb *make* to form a phrase. The phrase is then inserted into the second sentence.]

GO ON

Developmental Language Skills

EXERCISE B Combine each of the following pairs of sentences. Take the underlined phrase from one sentence and insert it into the other sentence. Be sure to add commas if they are needed.

Examples 1. The new library will open on Saturday. It is a <u>large, modern building</u>. [The phrase *a large, modern building* is taken from the first sentence and inserted into the second.]
The new library, a large, modern building, will open on Saturday.

2. The ducks stay together. They are <u>swimming on the lake</u>. [The phrase *swimming on the lake* is taken from the first sentence and inserted into the second.] *The ducks swimming on the lake stay together.*

6. The painting is <u>by Theresa</u>. That painting is beautiful. [Where should the underlined phrase be inserted in the second sentence?] _____

_____

7. My father bought a new lawnmower. He will <u>cut the grass</u> with it. (Add *to*.) [Where should the newly formed phrase be inserted in the first sentence?] _____

_____

8. Our dog has long, floppy ears. His name is <u>Mr. Sampson</u>. _____

_____

9. The old house is for sale. The house is <u>on the corner</u>. _____

_____

10. The Riveras moved <u>in early 1999</u>. The Riveras moved into the neighborhood. _____

_____

11. Mr. Peterson grows many colorful flowers. He is <u>our next-door neighbor</u>. _____

_____

12. My new sweater is very warm. It is <u>made of wool</u>. _____

_____

13. The circus <u>travels around the country</u>. The circus just arrived in town. (Change *travels* to *traveling*.) _____

_____

14. My sister is saving money. She will <u>buy a new computer</u> with the money she saves. (Add *to*.)

_____

15. The students are <u>enrolled in the art class</u>. The students will meet in the library today. _____

_____

HOLT HANDBOOK | First Course

Combining Sentences by Using *And*, *But*, or *Or*

You can link ideas of nearly equal weight to combine sentences. With the words *and*, *but*, and *or*, you can make a compound subject, a compound verb, or a compound sentence.

When two sentences have the same verb but have different subjects, you can join the subjects to make one sentence. When you join the subjects, you form a *compound subject.*

SAME VERB	The cement truck **drove** into the parking lot. The dump truck **drove** in, too.
COMPOUND SUBJECT	**The cement truck and the dump truck** drove into the parking lot. [The subjects *cement truck* and *dump truck* are joined by *and* to make a compound subject.]

When two sentences have the same subject but have different verbs, you can make one sentence with a *compound verb.*

SAME SUBJECT	**The cement truck** drove into the parking lot. **The cement truck** did not stay long.
COMPOUND VERB	The cement truck **drove** into the parking lot **but did** not **stay** long. [The verbs *drove* and *did stay* are joined by *but* to make a compound verb.]

EXERCISE A Use proofreading marks to combine each of the following sentences. You may need to change the form of a verb to agree with a compound subject.

Examples 1. French I ~~was~~ offered last year. ~~Spanish I was offered, too.~~ [*and Spanish I were*] [Both sentences have the same verb, *was offered*. *And* is used to combine the two different subjects. The verb *was* is changed to *were* to agee with the compound subject.]

2. Dad could fix the problem. ~~He~~ doesn't have any metric tools. [*but*] [Both sentences have the same subject, *Dad. But* is used to combine the two different verbs.]

1. Shall we save these? Shall we throw them out? [Do both sentences have the same subject? Which words should be used to join the two sentences?]

2. Baseball cards can be quite valuable now. Basketball cards can be, too. [Do both sentences have the same verb? Which word should be used to join the two sentences?]

3. These lightbulbs burn brightly. They emit little heat.

4. Taylor's Music may have that CD. Music Incorporated may have it, too.

5. Lake Maracaibo is South America's largest lake. It serves as a major port with ocean access.

6. Everybody has signed up for the field trip. Tim has not signed up yet.

7. Radar is scanning the area now. It is not registering anything.

8. The foundation of the new house will be completed by then. The frame will been completed, too.

9. That little wooden puzzle looks easy. It isn't.

10. Erosion may have caused that formation. Volcanic activity may have done so, too.

Often, two sentences will have different subjects and different verbs. When two such sentences are closely related, you can combine them to make one sentence called a *compound sentence*.

    ORIGINAL   A worker waved. The cement truck backed into the parking lot.

    COMBINED   A worker waved**, and** the cement truck backed into the parking lot.

EXERCISE B Use the words *and, but,* or *or* to combine each of the following pairs of sentences. Remember that you may need to change capitalization and to delete or add words. Write your answers on the lines provided.

Example 1. The elephant herd set off for the river. The baby elephant had other ideas. [*But* can

    be used to make a compound sentence.] *The elephant herd set off for the river, but*

    the baby elephant had other ideas.

11. Fireflies flitted in the darkness. We watched them for a long time. [Which word would be best

to join the two sentences?] _____

_____

12. Strangely enough, the Cherokee rose originated in China. These flowers now flourish in the

southern states. _____

_____

13. Our club is cleaning the vacant lot next to the school. We are planting trees there as well. _____

_____

14. Did you call Mary this morning? Should I do it? _____

_____

15. Jim wanted to see the play at the Alley Theater. He could not catch the bus on time. _____

_____

Combining Sentences Using Subordinate Clauses

Adjective Clauses

An **adjective clause** is used to describe a noun or pornoun. You can combine sentences by turning one sentence into an adjective clause and inserting it into another sentence. Usually, you will need to add a word, such as *who, that,* or *which,* at the beginning of the adjective clause.

> **ORIGINAL** The director made this film. He is now quite famous.
>
> **COMBINED** The director **that made this film** is now quite famous. [The two original sentences are combined to make one complex sentence. The word *that* introduces the adjective clause.]

EXERCISE A Combine each of the following pairs of sentences by turning one sentence into an adjective clause. Remember that you may need to add, delete, or change words. Write your combined sentences on the lines provided.

Example 1. We need someone. The person can talk to anyone. [The second sentence can be turned into an adjective clause. The word *who* is used introduce the adjective clause.]

We need someone who can talk to anyone.

1. His watch alarm suddenly went off. It had been programmed by his computer. [Which word in the first sentence does the second sentence describe?]

   _____

   _____

2. The tune stays with me to this day. The tune was a Mexican folk song. [Which word in the first sentence does the second sentence describe?]

   _____

3. Every single night, the only book is *Madeline.* My little sister wants it read to her. _____

   _____

4. Finally we had gotten every mosquito except for a few. A few got away. _____

   _____

5. Ask for directions from the park ranger. He is wearing the red cap. _____

   _____

GO ON ➡

Adverb Clauses

Adverb clauses describe verbs, adjectives, or adverbs. An adverb clause begins with a word such as *after, before, while, until, unless, when, where, wherever,* or *although,* which tells the reader how the idea in the adverb clause relates to the rest of the sentence.

ORIGINAL	The director made this film. He was very young.
COMBINED	**When the director made this film,** he was very young. [The first sentence was turned into an adverb clause. The word *When* introduces the adverb clause.]
ORIGINAL	His whole life changed. The film was released.
COMBINED	His whole life changed **after the film was released.** [The second sentences was turned into an adverb clause. The word *after* introduces the adverb clause.]

EXERCISE B Combine each of the following pairs of sentences. Use the word in parentheses to turn one of the sentences into an adverb clause. Remember that you may need to add, delete, or change words and punctuation. Write your combined sentences on the lines provided.

Example 1. The tower radioed the pilot. The pilot taxied onto the runway. (Use *when.*) [The first sentence is turned into an adverb clause. The word *When* introduces the adverb clause.]

When the tower radioed the pilot, he taxied onto the runway.

6. Hang the clothes on the line. The washing machine is finished. (Use *after.*) [Which sentence can be changed into an adverb clause?]

_____

_____

7. Joe unloaded the truck. Alison got a signature on the delivery receipt. (Use *while.*)

_____

_____

8. Look people in the eye and shake hands. You meet them. (Use *when.*) _____

_____

9. I had never been to a museum. I came here last year. (Use *before.*) _____

_____

10. You can read your assignment. The dryer is running. (Use *while.*) _____

_____

Revising Stringy Sentences

Identifying Stringy Sentences

A *stringy sentence* is made up of several complete thoughts strung together with words like *and* or *but*.

> **STRINGY SENTENCE** Mario likes cars, and Jill likes computers, and they would like to design cars on a computer, but they don't have a computer, do you? [This sentence is stringy. It uses *and* twice and *but* once to string together several complete thoughts.]

Stringy sentences just go on and on. When you read a stringy sentence, break it up. Your first step is to find each complete thought. How many complete thoughts are there in the stringy sentence above?

> **COMPLETE THOUGHTS** Mario likes cars.
>
> Jill likes computers.
>
> They would like to design cars on a computer.
>
> They don't have a computer.
>
> Do you have one?

EXERCISE A For each of the following items, underline each complete thought. Do not underline words such as *and, but, or, so, for,* and *yet* when they join complete thoughts.

Example 1. <u>I typed in my question</u>, and <u>I pressed the Enter key</u>, and <u>the computer made a noise</u>, but <u>nothing else happened</u>. [There are four complete thoughts. Each one has its own subject and verb.]

1. The rangers followed the tracks of the mountain lion, and she had gone down the mountain to the stream, and her tracks led back up into the rocks, and, there, the rangers lost her trail. [The four subjects are *rangers, she, tracks,* and *rangers.*]

2. They were sitting in an outside restaurant, and a waiter was carrying a tray with six full glasses on it, and a lady with a scruffy, little dog on a leash came in, and you can guess the rest of this sad tale.

3. Eventually, the police charged Goldilocks with unlawful entry, and they should have charged her with theft, but Mrs. Bear felt sorry for the girl, and the Bear family dropped the charges.

4. The alley was extremely narrow, and the garbage truck backed up, but there wasn't enough room, and the truck knocked over three full cans, and the driver just left them there.

5. I had never been in such a big hotel before, so I had not expected it to be so big, but it was beautiful, and it had a garden right in the lobby, and it had a fountain with fish in it, too.

Revising Stringy Sentences

Once you have found the complete thoughts in a stringy sentence, you're ready for the next step. The next step is breaking up the sentence. You may need to add, change, or take out words. You may want to join thoughts that are closely related and separate one that are not. Make sure that your new sentences sound express complete thoughts and do not sound choppy. When you are finished, check your capitalization and punctuation. Remember that it is perfectly fine to have two complete thoughts separated by a word such as *and, but,* or *or.* Just be sure to avoid three or more.

STRINGY SENTENCE   Mario likes cars, and Jill likes computers, and they would like to design cars on a computer, but they don't have a computer.

IMPROVED SENTENCES   Mario likes cars. Jill likes computers. They would like to design cars on a computer, but they don't have one.

OR

Mario likes cars, and Jill likes computers. They would like to design cars on a computer. However, they don't have a computer.

EXERCISE B Each of the following items contains a stringy sentence. Use proofreaders' marks to break each stringy sentence into clear, smooth sentences. Be sure to check capitalization and punctuation.

Example 1. As We went up to the second floor of the building, and suddenly I heard my name so I looked around and down, and there was Louie on the ground floor. [The revised first sentence now has only one complete thought: *I suddenly heard my name.* The second sentence has two complete thoughts that are closely related: *I looked around and down* and *there was Louie on the ground floor.*]

6. Mountain goats watched the climber, but the climber was concentrating on his ropes, and he didn't see the goats. [What are the complete thoughts?]

7. Danny gave Ruben the money for a concert ticket, and so did Annie and then Ruben bought the tickets for everyone.

8. Put the egg in a bowl and beat it with a little water and then slowly add the flour and salt and mix again.

9. Mom and Dad usually go out on Friday, and I stay home and watch my little sister, but last Friday, we all went out to dinner.

10. A clown was selling balloons, and we watched him make balloon animals, and there were children crowding all around him.

Revising Wordy Sentences

Have you ever had to listen to a speech that just went on and on and on? It wasn't much fun, was it? Perhaps the speaker used several words where one would do.

Writing or speaking that contains unnecessary words is called *wordy*. Wordiness can confuse your audience or cause them to lose interest. When you take out extra words, you can strengthen your writing or speaking by making your points more effectively.

This worksheet shows you three ways to revise wordy sentences.

First Strategy: Replace a phrase with one word.

> **WORDY**   Mr. Ash is for all practical purposes an expert at appliance repair.
>
> **REVISED**   Mr. Ash is **practically** an expert at appliance repair.

> **WORDY**   Mr. Ash is an expert at just about any kind of appliance repair.
>
> **REVISED**   Mr. Ash is an expert at **all kinds** of appliance repair.

EXERCISE A Each of the following sentences is wordy. Cross out any extra words or phrases. If necessary, write in a word to replace them.

Example 1. ~~With a sudden motion,~~ *Suddenly* she reached out and caught an apple in midair. [The phrase

With a sudden motion can be replaced with the word *Suddenly.*]

1. As a result of the fact that there was a delay, travelers were camped out all over the airport.

[What is one word that can replace *As a result of the fact that*?]

2. In a state of excitement, Jane called her mother to tell her the news.

3. In spite of the fact that Sandra had the time, she did not want to go to a movie.

4. At the time at which that show begins, will you let me know?

5. Given the fact that the museum is closed, perhaps we should take a walk around the lake.

Second Strategy: Take out *who is* or *which is.*

> **WORDY**   Mr. Ash, who is our neighbor, is an expert at appliance repair.
>
> **REVISED**   Mr. Ash, **our neighbor,** is an expert at appliance repair.

> **WORDY**   Appliance repair, which is a valuable skill, requires experience.
>
> **REVISED**   Appliance repair, **a valuable skill,** requires experience.

EXERCISE B Each of the following sentences is wordy. Cross out any extra words or phrases. If necessary, write in a word to replace them.

Example 1. My presentation will be on King Tut, ~~who was~~ the topic of my research project. [The

words *who was* are unnecessary.]

6. King Tut, who was a young pharaoh of Egypt, remains a popular subject. [Which words can be crossed out?]

7. His tomb, which was one of the great finds of the twentieth century, contained many wonderful objects.

8. You have probably seen his gold mask, which is only one of the many magnificent treasures of the tomb.

9. Howard Carter, who was a British archaeologist, is famous for the discovery of the tomb.

10. The tomb was found in the Valley of the Kings, which is an area near Thebes.

Third Strategy: Take out a whole group of unnecessary words.

> **WORDY**   Mr. Ash really is pretty much of an expert at appliance repair.
>
> **REVISED**   Mr. Ash is **an expert** at appliance repair.
>
> **WORDY**   Mr. Ash can repair any kind of appliance that you can imagine.
>
> **REVISED**   Mr. Ash can repair any kind of appliance.

EXERCISE C Each of the following sentences is wordy. Cross out any extra words or phrases. If necessary, write in a word to replace them.

Example 1. ~~The reason why~~ I chose to take tennis ~~is~~ so that I can join a league next spring. [The words *The reason why* and *is* are not necessary. When these words are deleted, the sentence still means the same thing.]

11. The guitarist played a folk song from the country of Brazil. [How can *from the country of Brazil* be shortened to only two words?]

12. Unfortunately, the game has been canceled due to the fact of rain.

13. Did the Wright brothers make the first airplane flight ever to be made by anyone in history?

14. That day, he was wearing a shirt of a green color.

15. Stonehenge has fascinated the world for a long time, actually for a number of centuries.

Varying Sentence Beginnings and Sentence Structure

Varying Sentence Beginnings

Basic English sentences begin with a subject followed by a verb and often with a few other words. This sentence pattern is correct, but it can become boring to a reader. Notice how uninteresting the following paragraph sounds.

> I approached the gym. I heard a loud roar rise up. A thousand voices were cheering all at once. I felt bad for being late to our high school's biggest basketball game of the year. I quickened my pace. I rushed to the gym. What could be happening on the court? I was impatient and energized at the same time. I darted into the gym. I wanted to see what was happening. I had to climb to the top of the bleachers. I could scan the entire court. I was thrilled to be there!

One way to make sure your writing is interesting is to vary sentence beginnings. Instead of starting each sentence with a subject followed by a verb, you can begin some sentences with other words, phrases, and clauses.

> **As I approached the gym,** I heard a loud roar rise up. A thousand voices were cheering all at once. **At first,** I felt bad for being late to our high school's biggest basketball game of the year. **Quickening my pace,** I rushed to the gym. What could be happening on the court? **Impatient and energized at the same time,** I darted into the gym. **To see what was happening,** I had to climb to the top of the bleachers. **From that vantage point,** I could scan the entire court. **Finally,** I was thrilled to be there!

EXERCISE A The following paragraph is not very interesting because almost all the sentences begin with their subjects. Revise the paragraph by adding a variety of sentence beginnings. Use proofreading symbols to show your revisions.

Example ~~It was~~ <u>At</u> 6:45 A.M. I got up. ~~I slipped~~ <u>Slipping</u> on some bluejeans and a T-shirt, I went into the kitchen.

    I got some orange juice. I fixed a bowl of cereal. I sat down at the table. My cat Raven jumped onto the table. His front paw knocked the juice cup onto the floor. I hadn't started breakfast yet. I had to mop the floor. I couldn't believe it. I cleaned up the mess on the floor. I quickly finished my cereal. I barely made it to the bus stop on time. I learned a lesson. You can't put cats and juice in the same room before 7:00 A.M.

Varying Sentence Structures

Varying sentence beginnings is one good way to make your writing interesting. Another good way to make your writing interesting is to use a variety of sentence structures.

For example, read the following paragraph. Notice that the writer uses only simple sentences that have the same structure.

> The banjo is a musical instrument. This instrument became popular in the United States in the nineteenth century. It is a stringed instrument. It combines a guitar neck with a body like a tambourine. It is played in folk and country music. My sister decided to play the banjo. She heard a famous banjo picker. She has become an enthusiastic banjo student. She practices night and day. She is good at picking. Picking is plucking the strings with one's fingers or with a pick. People cannot help but dance. Banjo players start playing.

Now read the revised paragraph. Notice how the writer has varied sentence structure to make the writing more interesting.

> The banjo is a musical instrument. *(simple)* It became popular in the United States in the nineteenth century. *(simple)* The banjo is a stringed instrument that combines a guitar neck with a body like a tambourine, and it is played in folk and country music. *(compound-complex)* My sister decided to play the banjo after she heard a famous banjo picker. *(complex)* Now she has become an enthusiastic banjo student, and she practices night and day. *(compound)* She is good at picking, which is plucking the strings with one's fingers or with a pick. *(complex)* People cannot help but dance when banjo players start playing. *(complex)*

EXERCISE B The following paragraph is not very interesting because it has only simple sentences. Revise the paragraph to include a variety of sentence structures. Use proofreading symbols to show your revisions.

Example My family enjoys spending time outdoors. We went on a hike. We started early
                        because
              Saturday morning. We wanted to have a full day.

We walked along the forest trail. There was a thick mist in the air. We could barely see twenty feet ahead of us. It was daylight. The sunlight barely broke through the mist. We heard a noise. I turned around. I discovered a squirrel. It had jumped onto a nearby branch. We continued on the trail for about several hours. The mist was beginning to clear. We reached a field. We could now see the rolling hills. They were far in the distance. There was a nice patch of dry grass nearby with a view of the valley. We decided to stop for a break. Later, we continued our hike through the forest.

Using Transitions

Imagine living in a town with no signposts—no street signs, no stop signs, no familiar red and green lights, no signs anywhere. Getting around town would be a confusing process. In the same way, a reader may be confused by a paragraph that has no transitions. In writing, transitions are words or phrases that help to connect ideas. Transitions guide readers from one idea to the next. For example, some transitions signal time or order. Others show the relationship of one sentence to another.

EXAMPLES   Our science class will do an experiment. **First,** we will get out our chemistry sets. [The word *First* is a signal that shows the order of a process.]

Aunt Meg could buy a bookshelf. **On the other hand,** she could build one herself. [The phrase *On the other hand* is a signal that shows a contrasting relationship of two sentences.]

Common Transitional Words and Phrases

also	another	as a result	at last
besides	consequently	eventually	finally
first	for example	for instance	furthermore
however	in fact	last	mainly
meanwhile	moreover	on the other hand	soon
then	therefore	though	thus

EXERCISE A   There are ten transitional expressions in the following paragraph. Underline each transitional expression.

Examples [1] This chemistry project is easy and fun. <u>As a result</u>, I think you'll find it interesting.

[The phrase *As a result* shows a cause relationship between the first two sentences.]

[2] Remember, <u>though</u>, that cleaning up is part of the project! [The word *though* signals a comparison between this sentence and the one that comes before it.]

There are many easy science projects. Many students especially enjoy making slimy concoctions. [1] One favorite, for example, involves only a few ingredients. [Which two words show that this sentence will give a specific example of something mentioned in the preceding sentence?] [2] In fact, these ingredients are easy to find. [Which two words signal an explanation of information from the preceding sentence?] [3] The resulting concoction won't hurt you, though it does taste awful. [4] First, get some cornstarch and a small bowl. [5] Then, put some cornstarch in the bowl. Slowly pour some water into the cornstarch. [6] Finally, stir the mixture. [7] Soon, you will see the mixture begin to thicken. [8] However, if the mixture isn't thick enough, add a bit more cornstarch. [9] On the other hand, if the mixture is too thick, add water. [10] You may add, also, some food coloring for variety.

GO ON ➡

As you have already learned, transitional words and phrases act as signposts. They help relate one sentence to another sentence or idea. Usually, you will find these words and phrases at the beginning of a sentence. However, they can appear in the middle or at the end of a sentence.

BEGINNING OF A SENTENCE   My dog can do tricks. **For example,** he can sit.

MIDDLE OF A SENTENCE   My dog can do tricks. He can, **for example,** sit.

END OF A SENTENCE   My dog can do tricks. He can sit, **for example.**

TIP▶ Make a list of transitional words and phrases. There are many besides the ones listed on this page. Then keep your list handy whenever you are writing.

EXERCISE B Write an appropriate transitional expression on each blank for the following sentences. You can use words from the list on this worksheet or other appropriate transitional words or phrases.

Example 1. Everyone in our club gets along most of the time. The last month of school,

_____*however*_____, was different. [*However* is an appropriate transition because it signals a

contrast between the two sentences.]

11. _____, there was some disagreement among the club members. Ever since then, our

club has been divided about some decisions to be made. [Think of a word or phrase that shows

time.]

12. Some of us wanted to spend our leftover dues money on a club dinner—_____, a

banquet at a restaurant.

13. The club dinner could be a fun way to celebrate the year. _____, we could save the

money for next year.

14. Saving the money for next year would be a responsible thing to do. Some of the members,

_____, did not like the idea because they won't be at this school next year.

15. _____, we came up with a compromise that pleased everyone. We decided to spend a

portion of the money on a party and to have the rest for the club's future activities.